Rocking Horse Sh*t

The Ultimate Problem-Solving Manual

D1699471

Rocking Horse Sh*t

The Ultimate Problem-Solving Manual

by

Pádraic Ó Máille

Smacht Publications
The Granary Suites
Dominick Street
Galway
Ireland
www.smacht.com

Ordering Information
Quantity sales:
Special discounts are available on quantity purchases by
corporations, associations, and others. For details, contact
the publisher at the address above.
Orders by trade bookstores and wholesalers:
Please contact Smacht Publications at Tel: +353 91 865340;
or visit www.smacht.com

A man visited his Doctor complaining of feeling stressed out, run down and at the end of his tether.

'I've just the cure for you,' replied the Doctor, an affable and caring man.

'I prescribe that you spend one full hour in the company of Joey the Clown at the local circus. It'll take your mind of your troubles, make you laugh like a baby and you'll depart feeling uplifted, energised and with a pep in your step. You wouldn't believe the number of my patients who swear by the healing properties of Joey the Clown. I rate him as the best 'Shrink' in town. But hurry now. The matinee begins in half an hour.'

'I am Joey the Clown,' replied the patient.

This book is dedicated to Joey the Clowns the world over.

To ordinary people – school children, exam takers, parents, business people, sales people, professionals, those who are falling into and out of love – to everyone who is expected to perform at their peak, even in the face of crippling fear, worry and despair.

Contents

Foreword

For the past twenty-five years Pádraic Ó Máille has travelled the highways and byways of Ireland and beyond – meeting, mentoring and motivating thousands of people. He is one of the most popular and beloved men I know.

As he journeys, he collects stories, parables and wisdom from likely and unlikely sources. He brings to mind the scholars who travelled around Ireland cataloguing nature, history and folklore. They were known locally as "Praegers" after Robert Lloyd Praeger. You can read about his travels in "The Way That I Went," an account of his lifetime's work.

The book you are reading is Pádraic's 'The Way that I Went" – wisdom gained from business leaders, fishermen, teachers and his indefatigable Uncle Stíofáin. He is familiar with an astonishing range of literature, and quotes freely and appropriately from some great minds and writers, but everything in this book, and there is a lot in it, is grounded in a bedrock of experience and common sense.

Anyone who has met Pádraic realizes very quickly what a generous soul he is. I have known him all my adult life and if I had to sum him up in one word I would say that he is kind. He is also funny, charismatic, lyrical and intelligent. However, he has helped so many people in so many ways you would have to say that kindness defines him.

So it seems all the more cruel that Pádraic should become ill with a fantastically rare condition. True to form, he put the ordeal to good use and forged this book from terrifying experiences and long dark nights. Into every life some rain must fall, and Pádraic has written the manual for difficult times. This manual manages to be profound, touching, very honest and easy to read.

I would recommend this book to students, patients, workers, business people and anybody who does their best yet encounters trouble on the way. Which I suppose means all of us. I can see readers coming back to it time and again as their lives grow.

Pádraic did not just have a rare condition, he is a rare and special person. As the song goes "He's a man you won't meet every day." His book is surely going to be a classic of its kind, and will be enjoyed by readers of every disposition for many generations.

Dr. Pat Harrold

Chapter 1
Manage Your Wild Horses

'Pádraic, I need you to call me,' was all it said on the voice message.

A fairly innocuous message if it had come from your mother or a client or even your bank manager.

Ominous in the extreme however, if it was from your cardiologist.

I replayed the message hoping I might have gotten it wrong.

'Pádraic, I need you to call me.'

It's amazing how powerfully and speedily the mind works to protect you from confrontation and conflict. It forcibly reminded me that I was driving to Thurles where I was presenting to sixty business people in two hours and that I needed to be utterly focused on the job at hand and I should ring my cardiologist after lunch.

I dithered. Decided to listen to the message again.

There was no doubting the tonality and cadence and timbre in that voice. There was kindness there, and caring too. There was also a distinct 'don't mess me about' intonation.

From another recess of my mind whispered an affirmation called 'D.I.N'.

'D.I.N.' is an acronym for 'Do It Now' and over the years I'd helped thousands of people to confront their procrastination by getting them to affirm 'Do It Now' when they felt like putting something off. It's probably the first thing I say to myself each morning when the alarm rings and one voice seductively suggests I press the snooze button. I've programmed myself to counter by declaring 'D.I.N.' and, once a champion snoozer, I now rarely have a problem getting up first thing in the mornings, whether I feel like it or not.

I mentally muttered 'D.I.N.,' pulled off the road, dialled the number and willed for all I was worth he was anywhere but at that number.

Same voice. Same tonality. Different words.

'Pádraic, you didn't score an 'A' in your cardiac MRI'.

On a different day, in a different context, I'd have loved that headline.

David Ogilvy, the undisputed guru of the advertising industry, counselled his designers to 'Spend 80% of the clients money on the headline!' More specifically, he believed a headline needed to fulfil four criteria: 1. Grab Attention. 2. Create Interest. 3. Stimulate Desire. 4. Get the client to take Action.

I don't know if they teach 'AIDA' in Medical School but my cardiologist had hit the bulls eye on all four.

In those few moments it had taken him to utter those words, my life seemed to stutter and stall and dangle in suspense. It appeared as if I had unlimited time to assimilate those words and their implications.

I recalled earlier that month his prognosis on the angiogram he had performed on me.

'Beautiful arteries Pádraic.'

'What does that mean,? I asked ignorantly.

'It means Pádraic that your coronary arteries that supply blood to your heart are working perfectly and you have no evidence of coronary artery disease.'

I got the message. He could use more words than were necessary but it was neither his style nor preference.

Now he was scoring me 'Less than an 'A' in my cardiac MRI.' It was subtle as a brick – saying nothing yet saying everything. I knew it could be 84% or 4%. It did provoke me to take action however, and ask the first of what would be dozens of hard and uncomfortable questions.

'What's the story?' What's not perfect?'

'The MRI has detected that you may have left ventricular non-compaction.'

I scribbled it down on the unopened front page of the Irish Times on the passenger seat. It meant nothing to me. I'd check it out later online and deal with it then.

'It's also detected a nodule or a mass on your right atrium.'

That meant a lot to me. It sounded exactly like cancer and I hadn't a clue how to deal with that.

'I've contacted the go to man in Ireland for this type of condition. He'll see you at 8 pm on Friday in the Blackrock Clinic.'

'Hang on a second.' I said with some assertiveness. 'I've a gig on Friday.'

He'd have been forgiven for telling me in his best Mrs. Browne Dublin accent that 'Denial isn't a river in Egypt' but he desisted. He paused for what seemed an eternity.

'I'll be there.' I said.

****

Gurtymadden, on the road to Thurles, is not the most salubrious of settings to receive life changing news. On that damp Tuesday morning there were no restaurants open to purloin a sugary latte. There were no counselling clinics to sequester advice on how best to respond to potentially fatal news. There was no bookshop to acquire a book on what to do when you find yourself in times of trouble.

The only things moving in Gurtymadden that bleak Tuesday morning were about twelve wild and untrained Connemara ponies frolicking in a paddock beside the roadside. They were being put through their paces by a slip of a girl who was in complete control of the madness and mayhem that prevailed all about her.

The ponies were exuberant, skittish and unpredictable. They pranced around the confined space of the paddock without apparent purpose or reason. Some were frantically charging the robust fences in an effort to escape and dander in different fields with sweeter and more tender grass. Others continued to gallop around in the same circle over and over again. Already you could see deep ruts and grooves appearing in the green meadow as the ponies aimlessly and heedlessly acted out on impulse. Others again were listless and apathetic and simply lay listlessly on scraw's of worn bedding missing the ruggedness and bleakness of Connemara where they'd spent the first three formative years of their life.

Not for long. Their trainer, at all of eight stone, was a consummate horse trainer. To her, each wild pony was a champion in disguise waiting to be developed and unleashed. Over the coming minutes she succeeded in transforming the behaviour and performance of many of those ponies.

She had neither whip nor spur – her only concession to technology was a narrow gap in a wall that separated her and a bale of sweet hay from the ponies. Addressing each pony individually she allowed some enter the gap to indulge in the hay. Others were given further 'feedback' before being allowed access. Others again were not permitted entry at all.

I marvelled at how, with time and Smácht (Irish word for discipline), she would have each of those ponies jumping gracefully and happily through hoops and over fences. Many would go on to travel the world and be feted and lauded for the unique and disciplined creatures that they will become.

My mind was no different to that paddock.

It had become one massive uncontrolled riot of panic.

Wild horses were running amok and right now there was no trainer to calm them, to control them, to tame them, to harness them or to develop them.

All my life I'd been a worrier.

As a kid I was terrorised by the boogie man lurking beneath my bed. As a teenager I despaired that girls would never talk to me. As a student I'd stressed about failing every exam I ever took. As a business person I'd agonised about business drying up and going broke.

With the passing of time, and the development of specific strategies, I'd succeeded in overcoming many of those worries, and had progressed to achieving a modicum of success in certain circles.

However, one bitch persisted in stalking me. From as far back as I can remember I've been terrified of dying.

I had some justification. My own father had died two months before I was born. A cousin of mine had been killed at eleven and at fifteen, a close friend of mine had died of a brain haemorrhage.

I'd pictured in vivid detail being assailed by every conceivable disease from A to Z and each year would present in front of my GP with a new imagined ailment.

And now, it seemed, the self-fulfilling prophesy had come to pass. I recalled a line from the bible 'And the thing I feared greatly has come upon me.'

I now had an industrial strength health problem to worry about.

My thoughts, like those wild ponies, began to charge out of control.

I'd heard it said that about 60,000 thoughts or impulses cross our minds each day. These are exactly like the Gurtymadden ponies – some are thoroughbreds and perfectly formed – abundant with possibility and capable of being trained to within an inch of their lives. Others, however, lack the breeding, the physique and the temperament to ever achieve greatness. More again are destructive, dysfunctional and delusionary.

As I watched that girl in that little gap she patrolled between the hay and the paddock I was reminded of the iconic writer and psychiatrist Viktor Frankl. Frankl had lost his wife and daughter to the Nazi's under the most heinous circumstances yet still succeeded in retaining his sanity and purpose for life. In his iconic book *'Man's Search for Meaning'* he concludes that 'Everything can be taken from a man but one thing: the last of the human freedoms—to choose one's attitude in any given set of circumstances, to choose one's own way.' He continues to say that 'Between stimulus and response, there is a space. In that space is our power to choose our response. In our response lies our growth and our freedom.'

The lesson of Gurtymadden was clear.

We always have the power to choose our thoughts.

The process of choosing your thoughts is equally simple. Stupid as it sounds, create a mental space to acknowledge and listen to each of your thoughts. The mere fact of slowing your thoughts down creates a semblance of order and calm and control. Then resolutely decide which thoughts you choose to enter your reality and similarly decide which thoughts you choose to ignore and dismiss.

The friskiest thought beating my door down right then was, 'You've got cancer. Get back to Galway quick and down six pints to calm your nerves.'

I paused, acknowledged and reassured that thought that it was indeed possible I had cancer, and I would confirm that one way or the other on Friday. In the meantime, however, I was going to usher it out of the 'paddock of my mind' and obstinately refuse to even think about it until Friday.

My next thought was equally as immediate and demanding. 'You're delivering a presentation on 'Positive Thinking' in Thurles in two hours where you're expected to light up the room. How are you going to pull yourself together for that when you'll probably be dead in three months?

I had to give that thought serious credit. I didn't have an answer. I sensed, however, the presence of another pony called Joey the Clown nuzzling at my fingers and I thought I heard him whisper.

'The show must go on. You'll be fine. Let go of the trapeze and trust.'

And it does. And it will. And every step along the way Joey the Clowns will emerge from the universal ether to help you and guide you if you're receptive and open to them.

Summary

When you find yourself in times of trouble be aware that your mind resembles a paddock of wild ponies – with thoughts that are skitterish, frantic and out of control. Remember too that you can always erect a little space where you can vet these thoughts and discipline them and ultimately develop them.

This simple process is the bedrock of modern psychotherapy.

My son Harry, an intrepid Liverpool fan, had given me a copy of Dr. Steven Peters wonderful book *The Chimp Paradox* early on in my 'Troubles.' Dr. Peters was widely acclaimed as the guru behind Liverpool's excellent season in 2013/2014.

Dr. Peters has concluded that your mind has at least two thinking machines that independently interpret your experiences: the frontal and the limbic. The frontal region is your conscious mind – your logical, rational and evidence-based centre. Your limbic, however, is your wild pony or chimp – that emotional component of your brain that is paranoid, catastrophic and irrational. It is constantly working and can simultaneously be both your best friend and your worst enemy.

It dates from prehistoric times when it's core function was to activate the 'Fight, flight or freeze' impulse. Those impulses were wholly appropriate and oftentimes life saving in that era. And while it can still serve to protect you, frequently it will cause you to experience unnecessary feelings of panic, being overwhelmed and despair.

And while it's difficult to control your chimp, it is possible to manage him or nurture him. 'Managing your impulsive, emotional chimp as an adult will be one of the biggest factors determining how successful you are in life,' according to Dr. Peters.

Acknowledging your wild ponies or chimp is the first step. Communicating and listening to them is step two. Reassuring them with logical and rational facts is step three.

Chapter 2
You Always Have Choices

I would have given anything to have been a doctor.

Well, not quite.

I'll never forget opening the letter from the CAO in the privacy of my old bedroom. The previous Wednesday I'd surprised everyone including myself by getting 56 points in the Leaving Certificate. If they held Medicine at last year's points I'd just about scrape in.

I felt lucky. I wasn't. I was offered my second choice. Commerce in UCG.

I reflected on it for a while. 'A 'wee' while,' as they in Donegal.

These were the days before Brian Lenihan Snr had kindly bestowed on the nation the philosophy of 'Mature Reflection,' and there were pints to be drunk and girls to be courted and a career in business to be envisioned. I couldn't burst through that bedroom door quick enough.

Needless to say I accepted what I was offered – Commerce in UCG.

Four of my friends also failed to get the points for Medicine in UCG that day. Interestingly, they're all doctors today.

Two of them chose to repeat the Leaving Certificate. The third guy took the scenic route and did a Bachelor of Science Degree and then got a concession into Medicine. The fourth person, if he was doing the Leaving until today, would still not have acquired the requisite 60 points entry level.

I recall vividly listening to him one night in the Cellar Bar in Galway prattling on about 'still doing Medicine despite the Leaving Cert results.' I felt compelled to spell it out for him. 'Look here Einstein' – he liked that – 'you need points to do Medicine in UCG. 60 of them. You're way off. It's impossible for you to become a doctor.'

In his stupidity he continued to affirm that he'd be 'a doctor someday.'

And he is. And a bloody good one. He discovered, through conscious choice and constancy of purpose, that qualification for Medicine in the UK was based on a combination of an interview for bedside manner and a certain modicum of academic points. He was more than suitably qualified. And so was I, had I known.

But back in 1979 no one had explained to me that life is a series of choices. My four buddies had consciously chosen to be doctors and chosen to pay in full the price that it required.

I, on the other hand, had chosen what society had offered me, and as such, unconsciously, had chosen by default.

****

It's said that 'those things that hurt, instruct,' and I must say, that the lesson of conscious choice had seldom been lost on me.

Even now, just minutes after getting news that I had a growth in my heart, I realised intuitively that I had a choice to make. I could return home and justifiably feel sorry for myself. Or I could continue on to Thurles and try and present to a group of business people as scheduled.

My thoughts – wild horses – were stampeding. I succeeded in slowing those thoughts down and entertaining them one at a time in the knowledge that the conscious mind can ever only deal with one thought at a time.

Most of the thoughts were negative in the extreme and counselled me to get my ass back to Galway pronto. I listened to them, acknowledged them and mostly agreed with them.

And in the midst of the mental carnage came the iconic words from The Beatles.

When I find myself in times of trouble
Mother Mary comes to me.
Speaking words of wisdom …

Except in my case it was my Aunty Mary. The kindest, wisest and most caring person you'd ever encounter. But instead of ending the verse with 'Let it Be,' she very clearly was saying to me.

'Do the right thing Pá because it's right.'

That philosophy or mindset was what I needed. I made a conscious choice to drive to Thurles and see how I felt when I got there.

****

The Conference Centre was one of the busiest in Ireland. This morning was no different. Each meeting room was packed to the gills with the good and great of corporate Ireland and at 11 am, they were now all spilling out for the ubiquitous 'elevenses'.

Even amidst the clutter and chaos, Logisticat stood out. Their corporate livery was crisp, punchy and well designed. Their team was actively working the room – making eye contact; shaking hands; looking after their guests. They served scones and cream as opposed to the standard hotel biscuits.

Everything about Logisticat exuded class. None more so than the presence of their founder, Jim Anderson.

I'd never met Jim.

This weekend I'd received a phone call from Jack Kennedy. Not a man given to superfluous talk, he had waxed lyrical for fifteen minutes on the exploits and achievements of his best friend Jim. He described how as, a young engineer, he had blazed a trail in Europe developing massive business for every company he worked for. Then, in 2005, he had set up Logisticat, and it was now a major player in the global logistics industry. He described Jim as being one of nature's great leaders.

Tragically, Jim passed on last Christmas at the young age of 45. The conference essentially was an opportunity for the company to meet its customers and reassure them of it's current status and future plans for the business. In keeping with the company ethos of quality and professionalism, a carefully prepared agenda had been agreed to impress and inspire their customers. It was to feature a number of technical inputs from the management team and conclude with an uplifting motivational address to send clients home in an upbeat and positive mood.

The motivational speaker was to have been an iconic former Tipperary hurling player and manager. Regrettably he had had a family bereavement at the last moment and was unable to perform the address. In a panic, Janet Anderson, Jim's wife had gotten my name from Jack Kennedy and we'd talked by phone the day before yesterday.

She was understandably very uptight about having someone she'd never met present to her best customers. And despite the best of reassurances, Janet still needed sanction from the Board to approve my candidacy. They had ratified that with a fair degree of nervousness only yesterday.

I instantly recognised the Chairman from his photo on the Web site. Together with Jim, he'd founded the company in 2007. He decked me too, presumably from my Web site, and he made a bee line for me.

Dermot Simpson was quietly spoken, deliberate and attentive to detail.

I am loud, spontaneous and as yet, hadn't even decided what I was going to talk about.

Despite our respective differences, we shared one thing in common. We were both consummate professionals. Intuitively we knew that the most critical factor right now was to make those customers feel special irrespective of our divergent personal styles.

'You'll be wanting to check if your PowerPoint is working Pádraic. Let me bring you in to Max Casey our IT Director.'

I'd witnessed far too many deaths by PowerPoint to be a fan of it and hadn't decided yet whether to use it or not. I decided, however, not to make an issue of it.

Max was rehearsing his presentation on the stage in the theatre. If Dermot was attentive to detail, Max was obsessive about it. He systematically flicked through slide after slide of evidence-based factual data on every conceivable logistical challenge. Proudly, he informed me that 'hard nosed empirical research' was what separated Logisticat from their competitors and his role was to provide it in abundance and share it with his customers.

When I asked him casually as to what he thought his customers would like to get from my presentation he responded emphatically. 'Gear and Facts.'

He informed me that the presentation before the break featured a demonstration of all their systems. In addition, their clients were some of the most successful people in the Logistics industry and that ultimately they were interested in facts about being more efficient, more effective and more productive.

The wild ponies in my mind proceeded to stampede and break out of the paddock.

- You've got a massive big growth in your heart and it could clot during your presentation and kill you on stage.
- You've got cancer and probably won't survive the summer.
- There's no way you'll get your head together and be able to speak for forty minutes.
- You've no 'Gear' – you don't even have a PowerPoint presentation.
- You know nothing about the logistics and these guys want 'Facts.'

– Kennedy will kill you if you're not spectacularly good.

In keeping with their culture of discipline and good time management, the meeting resumed. The Chairman announced that Max would speak for thirty minutes and I would follow for forty minutes.

Those thirty minutes were amongst the longest of my entire life. As the fuller implications of what had been broken to me earlier that morning began to register, I descended into a deep pit of fear and desolation and self-pity. The wild ponies were footloose and on the rampage again and if I was to compose myself to speak, they had to be reined in and managed again.

I listened to the uproar in my head with mounting alarm and considered my choices. There really seemed to be only two. I could apologise to the Chairman, tell him the genuine truth, and decline to speak based on reasonably justifiable grounds of trauma and anxiety. Or I could attempt to speak and in all probability make a pig's ear of it.

I resorted this time to doing what weak people the world over do when faced with challenging choices. I did nothing. I chickened out of making any choice and as such 'chose by default.' I recalled Brian Tracy once saying that 'You're always choosing. The simple act of 'not choosing' is in itself a choice.'

Max concluded with a summary slide of all his slides and the Chairman called for questions. To my utter astonishment, question after question emerged from the floor. Max was right. This audience loved facts and he indulged them further in some of the finer points of 'integrated mono logistical systems.' There was warm applause on his conclusion.

I saw a text flash on my mobile phone from Jack Kennedy. 'No pressure P but this is a really important presentation. I'll be expecting an extra special performance.' If he only knew.

The Chairman introduced me by reading a typed biographical profile he'd downloaded from my Web site. Factually correct. Inspirationally anaemic. I was certainly no Celebrity Star. And the audience responded in kind. With a quiet and polite hand clap.

The audience were scattered roughly ten abreast in six rows descending theatre like to the floor. They were quiet, polite and waiting.

And there they were. In the bottom row. Centre aisle. Janet Anderson was class personified. Her designer dress was dark and demure. Respectably mournful yet elegantly classic. Her stylish hair was tinged with the faintest hue of natural grey that only people of real confidence and presence can wear.

She smiled encouragingly but no amount of faking could disguise the fear and apprehension in that smile. A short few months, ago she had blissfully managed the family dimension of Jim Anderson's life leaving him free to do what he did best – develop a global business. Today, like it or like it not, she'd be expected to present the public face of Logisticat without Jim. And right now, more than anything else, she needed me to make a good impression.

Jason sat to the right of his mother with all the demeanour of a mature adult, yet barely seventeen. His eye contact was steady, interested and warm.

In another week, Jason would finish his Transition Year. In a perfect world, he should be dreaming about mornings in bed; the World Cup; and girls. And whilst in due course that will happen, today the boy had been catapulted into an adult's world. A world where he was expected to look good, sound good and perform.

And in that instant, I was struck by the difference between age and maturity. To age is inevitable and inexorable. It's physical. It simply happens. Everyone ages. Even Madonna has aged. And Obama too. Even Oisin aged after falling in Tír na Nóg. There's little achievement in ageing.

To mature, however, is far from being a fait accompli. It demands emotional intelligence. It requires becoming consciously aware of your choices in every moment of your existence. Mature people consciously and repeatedly choose their response to circumstances. Mature people choose to be graceful under pressure and as such they lead the world.

In short, mature people and organisations take responsibility for their results.

Like Janet and Jason, I too could, and would, perform at my best for forty minutes. I could focus 100% on that audience and I could consign any morbid or negative thoughts or feeling sorry for myself for another time.

In a nanosecond, I went from desperation to inspiration.

Ignoring any PowerPoint I began by saying. 'Max tells me you love facts and gear. Today, I want to talk to you about some mental facts and the gear you need to deal with them.'

I went on to reveal that in Ireland today there are 400,000 people on antidepressants with the figure projected to rise to 600,000 by 2020. I discussed some alarming American findings that disclose that 80% of new businesses go bankrupt within five years. And I revealed that what David Thoreau concluded in 1850 is still true in that '60% of us lead lives of quiet desperation and are less than happy with the careers we have.'

I then proceeded to give them some decent practical strategies to confront and cope with those three issues.

I knew a thing or two about Munster audiences. They don't do instant intimacy. They like to see you earn your corn before warming and responding to you. But if you're prepared to hang on in there and give it a decent shot there's no more better audience in the land.

For those forty minutes, I forgot about the growth in my heart and focused on the fire in my heart. It worked like a dream. The crowd caught on and joined in. I only have three funny stories in my repertoire. As a minimum standard of performance, I always try to get one in. That day, I succeeded in getting all three in.

Summary

1. Montaigne fairly nailed it when he said, 'Choice, not chance, determines destiny.' Like it, or like it not, you are always choosing. You are either doing this consciously, unconsciously, or someone else is choosing for you. The key takeaway from this chapter is to become a proactive or conscious choice maker. Brian Tracy is on the money when he says, 'You are always free to choose what you do first, what you do second, and what you choose not to do at all.'

2. 'Do the right thing because it's right' is the filter or benchmark to run your choices by. Doing the right thing will frequently not be the easiest, most desirable or popular choice – but ultimately, you will come to appreciate that what Harry Potter was told in *The Chamber of Secrets* is true. 'It is our choices, Harry, that show what we truly are, far more than our abilities.'

3. Remember that there's a massive difference between age and maturity. Francis Bacon once said. 'A person that is young in years may be old in hours if they've lost no time.' Maturity is a direct function of taking responsibility for your choices in life. There's a little tension brewing between academic and business circles currently. For years the academic community prided itself on the concept of IQ, or Intellectual Quotient. It

measured intellectual intelligence and was proven to be largely genetic and fixed. In recent times, the concept of EQ, or Emotional Intelligence has emerged and it's been proven that 90% of all successful CEOs have high levels of EQ but not necessarily IQ. EQ, or 'maturity', is the fundamental characteristic of all high performers. And the good news is that's it's neither genetic or fixed. It's learnable. Your choice.

4. Woody Allen once said that 'Showing up is 80 percent of life. Sometimes it's easier to hide home in bed. I've done both.' Winners don't show up only when they're strong and powerful and dangling a Honey on their arm. They show up when they're knackered and beaten and their nearest and dearest have abandoned and lost faith in them. Instinctively they know that success is ultimately a numbers game and that failure and success are the twin sides of the one coin. I love the story of Therese Maher and the 2013 All Ireland Winning Galway Camogie Team. Therese had shown up for Galway for each of the last sixteen years, including playing in five finals, and losing each time. Now, and forever more, she's an All Ireland Champion. We too can become champions by choosing to show up, whether we feel like it or not. To show up for our children, our communities, our customers, our country - ourselves. That's showing up. It's a conscious choice. A mature choice.

5. I heard Stephen Covey tell a story in Dublin once that blew my mind. He described getting into an empty carriage of a train early one Sunday morning. Every-

thing was quiet and peaceful until at the next stop a man got in with four kids and they were going ballistic. What was worse was that the man didn't even seem to notice. He did nothing to intervene. Covey made a conscious choice. He decided to politely inform the man that his kids were creating a scene and asked him if he could control them. The man apologised and explained that, 'They're mother died just three hours ago and I don't know how best to deal with them.' Covey said he experienced for the first time what a 'paradigm shift' was. He said the entire carriage – which moments earlier had been furious – were now offering sympathy and help and support to the family. You too can induce a paradigm shift in your life by focusing less on yourself and more on other people. It's another mature choice.

6. Ralph Waldo Emerson, one of my favourite writers of all time, counselled to 'Do the thing you fear and the death of fear is certain.' This is such a gem of wisdom that we'll devote an entire chapter to it later but there's nothing to prevent you starting it today.

7. Focus on the fire in your heart as opposed to the fear in your mind. To repeat once again, your conscious mind is only ever capable of entertaining one thought at a time. As Les Brown says 'You can either live your dreams or you can live your fears.' Sounds like another conscious choice.

8. And be aware, that at 17 or 53 or any age, the show goes on.

Chapter 3
All You Need is Smácht

Lest I needed reminding, the unopened copy of the Irish Times lay strewn across the passenger seat of the car. Scrawled in my own writing were the words my cardiologist had issued me over the phone. 'Mass or nodule on right atrium.'

Connecting with an audience of sixty people had helped distract from the very real issue scribbled on that paper. Now I was alone in the car. Or more precisely, my nodule and I were alone in the car. It felt like I'd just picked up an unwelcome hitchhiker and the mood in the car was strained, uncomfortable and a tad hostile.

Aimlessly I manoeuvred the car through Templemore and on up towards Roscrea. My wife was away shopping in Dublin for the day and I dreaded the notion of returning to an empty house. When I saw the signpost for Mount Saint Joseph Monastery, I thought it a serendipitous sign direct from The Lord himself.

My father-in-law, quite the holiest and most spiritual person I'd ever met, despaired of the infamous Galway Novena where, annually, up to 25,000 people stampede the Galway Cathedral in search of instant gratification. He referred to it as 'plastic religion' where an expectation was created that you could generate miracles by prattling off a series of prayers from a holy looking booklet. 'You can't turn God on and off like a tap,' he'd remonstrate. 'You shouldn't expect to pass your exams simply by rhyming off a novena if you haven't the work done.' He believed firmly that in life you reaped what you sowed.

I knew where he was coming from but I'd always been a bit of a 'plastic Jesus' myself. During times of imminent trouble like sitting exams or meeting the bank manager or addressing a really hostile audience, I'd always resort heavily to God. And then, in times of peace and stability, I'd forget all about him. Now that I was in serious trouble again, I figured it was well worth a call on the Monastery.

The Monastery hadn't changed an iota since I'd first entered it as a student in the adjoining boarding school forty years ago. It was imposing then and equally so now. The first thing that struck me always upon entering was the sheer height of the domed ceilings and vaults. I recall Fr. Dermot reverently explaining to us that therein was the magic of Gothic architecture – 'it leads the eyes upwards towards The Lord.' My problem with this was that it always induced within me a mild state of vertigo and I invariably found myself lowering my gaze to focus on more lowly things. Forty years ago that would most likely have been on the girls from the local convent in the pews in front.

Today, however, I was fully intent on connecting with God. I prayed with intensity and ardour and enthusiasm but to little avail. As if to defy me, the church began to crank up the volume in preparations for Vespers. A few very old monks began to shuffle in to take their place and get a few quick prayers in before the ceremony. I figured they must be very close to God. They were followed by Fr. Gabriel on the organ. Now in his eighties, he could still make every brick in the Monastery resonate to the warmth of that organ. And then the chanting commenced. There's something hypnotic about Gregorian chant.

You'd think with all that divine ambience that I'd have surely received some divine intervention to comfort me in my travails. It wasn't to be. The Divine WiFi was down. I departed midway through the 'Gloria' feeling more dejected and depressed than entering. 'So much for serendipity,' I thought despairingly to myself closing the massive wooden Monastery door.

And there he was. Brendan O'Rourke. Out for an afternoon stroll.

Nowadays he's best known to thousands of TV viewers as TG4's face and voice and sage of horse racing. To the hundreds of kids he taught in the 80s and 90s, however, he will be best remembered as an outstanding teacher and mentor and philosopher. Although his subjects were Irish and English, mostly he taught confidence and communication skills.

I should know better than most. In 1973, I came 47th in the entrance exam to Roscrea. That was precipitously close to the acceptance cut of 55 and clearly put me in the 'C' class. That did wonders for both my confidence and communications skills. Suffice to say, they were rock bottom. With Brendan's input I gradually moved up the grades finishing in the 'A' class and almost getting maximum points in Irish and English in the Leaving Cert at a time when 'A's in English and Irish were hard to get.

Over the years, we past students had often debated precisely what his magic was. It wasn't hard work. His classes were notoriously unstructured in that they frequently involved debates amongst ourselves.' It wasn't his academic background. Some other teachers had MA degrees but failed utterly to match Brendan's success as a teacher.

Brendan had what my mother would call 'maturity,' or a psychologist might call 'emotional intelligence,' or what the guy on the street would call 'cop on.' Intuitively he knew when to shut up and when to intervene. In business circles, it's said that 'feedback is the breakfast of champions.' Brendan did it better than almost anyone I knew. And his feedback was of both the positive and negative varieties. Brendan, like his county man Páidí Ó Sé who would subsequently coin the phrase, understood implicitly the psychological 'distance between a pat on the back and a kick in the ass.'

'You were saying a few prayers Pádraic!'

It was quintessential Brendan. A question disguised in a statement. I could say as much as I wanted, or as little. We began walking and I blubbered the lot out. Like all great listeners, he said nothing. And for the first time that day I began to come to terms with what I was facing. And it wasn't nearly as overpowering as it had seemed that morning.

He heard me out without interruption. It's still one of the greatest gifts we can bestow on another and a skill rarely taught in even our most prestigious universities.

I needed more than just being listened to, however. I needed wise and solid and practical advice. He seemed to sense this and quietly suggested to me that I had within myself the instrument of my cure.

'Pádraic, the answer to your greatest challenges always lie within you.'

I was cynical. As far as I was concerned, all that lay inside me was a growth in my right atrium that was in all likelihood boring a cancerous route through my lungs and throughout my entire body even as we spoke.

'In fact, I know what the answer to your problem is.'

I was curious.

'All you need to solve your current predicament is Smácht.'

In a previous chapter, I shared with you the acronym 'AIDA' beloved by David Ogilvy to recall the four components of all great communication messages. They need to grab Attention; stimulate Interest; create Desire; and get the listener to take Action.

Brendan had succeeded with the first two – Attention and Interest. Regrettably these were followed by Disappointment and Anger.

Smácht is a wonderful Irish word for discipline or manners or control. In addition, it was also the title of a business and personal development course I had developed with a certain modicum of success. However, I failed to see the relevance of how Smácht could solve my current plight.

'For Christ's sake Brendan, how can Smácht cure a growth in my heart?'

'Smácht is the solution to everything Pádraic.' Pointing at the school behind us he explained. 'Smácht is the secret to creating and sustaining a great school. Furthermore, it is the secret behind every successful organisation, business and country.'

'I know that Brendan.' I replied shirtily. 'But right now I need a fricking miracle not a philosophy.'

'Smácht is also the science behind miracles.'

'Says who?' And then I regretted saying it.

'I think you of all people can answer that Pádraic.'

He was right of course. I'd researched the subject extensively. All the great minds had in one way or another demonstrated that discipline, or Smácht, is key to success in any endeavour. M. Scott Peck, the iconic psychiatrist who wrote *The Road Less Travelled*, claimed on page one of that book that

> *Without discipline you cannot solve any problem. With some discipline, you can solve some problems. With total discipline, you can solve all problems.*

Newton's Laws of Motion are all based on it. His First Law states that 'An object at rest will remain at rest unless acted on.' Often referred to as the Law of Inertia, it suggests that if you do nothing, nothing happens. It takes Smácht to do something. His Third Law of Motion states that 'For every action there is an equal and opposite reaction.' This suggests that the quality of your action is critical. Once again, the quality of your consistent actions is a direct function of Smácht or discipline. If you exercise well (action) you will end up with a well-toned body (equal and opposite reaction).

The most definitive study undertaken on the correlation between Smácht and subsequent performance began in the 1960s, and involved monitoring the responses of young children to a stimulus. Popularly referred to as the Marshmallow Test, it gave kids the choice of getting one marshmallow now or getting two if they waited for a period of fifteen minutes.

What's fascinating is that the children who had the self-control to delay gratification succeeded much better in every aspect of life. They fared better at school; were socially more adept; and earned significantly more. Walter Mischel, who initiated the research, and continues to monitor the results, has concluded empirically that there is a direct link between Smácht and success.

I realised instinctively that Brendan was right and that if I was to have any chance of managing this unforeseen challenge, I'd have to be disciplined. Disciplined in:

My focus	S.H.A.G.
My thoughts	Mindset
Following up on my commitments	Accountability
How, and who I communicated with	Communications
My habits	Habits
My time	Time

Smácht is also an acronym for the above areas of discipline. Brendan launched a book of mine and was familiar with what each letter represented.

'What's your S.H.A.G. as of today Pádraic?'

S.H.A.G. is an acronym for 'Smácht Hairy Accountable Goal' and represents what is the most important goal in your life currently. Up to now, mine had been very clearly a business goal.

Very quickly, without any thought, I was able to tell him.

'My S.H.A.G. is to live a totally healthy life.'

'Maith a' bhuachaill. What Mindset would serve you best in order to achieve a totally healthy life?

Once again, the answer was immediate, and required no thinking.

'I need a Mindset of Smácht to achieve my S.H.A.G.'

'Well done, but actions speak louder than words. How, and who, will you be accountable for achieving your S.H.A.G.?

I told him I needed to think more about that but would revert to him when I had.

'Who are the most important people you have to communicate with about this news, and how best will you do this?

It instantly occurred to me what a shock this would be for my wife when she heard it this evening. There were two ways I could present it – one, in a state of panic and two, in a state of control. The latter would require Smácht, but it was the right thing to do. I mentally began to scope out the other discrete groups of people I would have to communicate with – my kids, my clients, my suppliers. I resolved to say as little as possible to my mother as she has a very negative predisposition.

'What Habits would best serve you in order to achieve your goal?

Instantly I realised that Smácht was a habit and the Daddy of all others, and even though I'd written the book on it, I wasn't its best practitioner. It occurred to me then that it would be important to continue exercising as that would impact my health and energy and healing. In addition, I would continue the habit of meditating.

Finally, Brendan asked me how best I would spend my time over the foreseeable future. I realised that this would need to change radically in the future. Once again, I told him I'd come back to him on that.

The bells of the Monastery peeled in the background signalling that it was 6 pm. The Divine WiFi had been working all the time.

Summary

1. The old adage still holds true. 'A problem shared is a problem halved.' Choose wisely who you share it with, however. The Brendan's of this world are exceptions. Most will prefer to tell you their problems and how much worse they were. Avoid people like this like the plague.

2. Listening to another person without interruption or evaluation is one of the greatest gifts you can bestow on another, and it's entirely free!

3. Smácht is all you need. Remember Newton's First Law however. 'An object at rest will remain at rest unless acted on.' Babies come hard wired with Smácht. They will fall dozens of times on their bums without giving up. As they grow older, however, they become seduced by a mindset called 'instant gratification.' This is the 'play now pay later' attitude that characterised much of the adult behaviour behind the creation of the Celtic Tiger. Smácht needs to be coaxed, cajoled, developed and nurtured. The good news is that it can. Ask anyone who's raised a happy child; run a marathon; or started a business. None are possible without Smácht.

4. Get a great S.H.A.G. It will provide you with focus, direction, passion and purpose.

5. You become what you think about most of the time. Are the horses in your mind wild and unruly or are they specimen thoroughbreds? The choice is yours. With Smácht, you can have the latter.

6. Weight-watchers know what they're about. What gets measured gets done. Start measuring your results in any area of your life and watch your performance soar.

7. 95% of your results in life come through communications with others. At no time is this more important than when you find yourself in times of trouble. Do yourself a favour. Get around positive people who uplift you and disassociate with emotional vampires –

people who suck the energy from you. Bear in mind that these people may be very close to you.

8. Dryden once said that 'First we make our habits. Then our habits make us.' Habits are the hardware of our minds. Becoming a slave to good habits is pure Smácht.

9. Your time is your life and the most valuable time is NOW – this present moment.

10. Whether you call it God; the Universal Intelligence; the Higher Power; Space; or 'Whatever You're Having Yourself', there's incontrovertible evidence that we've come from someplace and we're going someplace. Something exists infinitely greater than ourselves and it can serve us if we have the Smácht to open to it.

Chapter 4
The Ultimate Worry
Formula

Maybe the MRI scan had got it wrong. Hopefully it would be something innocuous. But then again, as I constantly harangued my clients, hope is not a strategy.

The cardiologist didn't beat about the bush. He was doing me a favour squeezing me in for a TOE (a transesophageal echocardiogram) at 8am on a morning he'd had other plans for.

In the pre-op suite he'd explained to me the 'good catch' that the radiology team had done in identifying the growth at all. It was inconclusive on the scan and would require inserting an ultrasound scanner down my oesophagus and into my stomach whereupon he could get a closer look at the growth.

Of course I should have asked him what he thought the growth was. How often do we quote Tim Ferriss at Smácht that 'A person's success in life can usually be measured by the number of uncomfortable conversations he or she is willing to have.' But I fudged it. Chickened out. Hoped again that it would be fine.

Only last weekend I'd been kite surfing in the waves in Lahinch, blissfully unaware of tumours in the heart. Afterwards I'd met my wife for lunch in Ballyvaughan and loitered with relaxation over the weekend newspapers for hours. That evening we'd had dinner in Linnanes and I got to sit in my favourite seat overlooking Galway Bay and the sun setting over Connemara and The Twelve Pins.

We luxuriated over plans for the first decent holiday of our adult lives. For the first summer in 25 years our kids were independent and we had planned to spend a full month chilling in the south of France from mid-June to mid-July. We'd purloined the ideal house – set on a cliff face overlooking the stunningly picturesque and historical town of Collioure.

And now, with two weeks to go I was supine on a bed in the Blackrock Clinic, answering a myriad of questions I'd answer a myriad of times over the coming months.

And then I was in theatre. A real live theatre.

As one of the nurses was helping me on to the operating table she burst out laughing.

'Would you look at yourself. Your gown is on back to front.'

I became terrified. And for the first time in four days, it wasn't the tumour that caused it.

'I'm grand and warm as I am,' I replied feebly, hoping she'd forget about it and get on with the procedure. I should have known better. You don't mess with a theatre nurse.

'Ah, we couldn't have you going back to the recovery room dressed like that. Put it on right now.'

Perched high upon the operating table I tried to be as inconspicuous as possible reversing that wretched surgical gown.

Once again, loud peals of laughter.

'Would you look at yourself. Are they your knickers you have on? They'll have to go. We may have to insert a tube up your groin.

Peripheral vision is amazing. Without turning my head I surveyed every conceivable hiding place in that theatre. There was none. It was bare, clinical, sterile. There was no place to hide. The guy who hid Shergar couldn't have hidden a pair of knickers in that theatre. They knew it. The anaesthetist knew it. And I knew it. And we all burst out laughing. No one had ever told me that you leave a certain bit of your dignity at the door of an operating theatre.

I went to sleep marvelling at how a sense of humour and cheerfulness and humanity can pervade and thaw even the most sterile of environments.

There wasn't much laughter upon awakening. The theatre was quiet, sombre, subdued. My cardiologist explained to me that there was indeed a growth on my right atrium and he'd already conferred with a cardiac surgeon about it. If I waited, the surgeon would talk to me following presently.

The wild horses in my mind were on the rampage again. They had almost reduced the guy who preached positive thinking for a living to a cathartic, miserable, hopeless bundle of nerves.

They would have too had my wife not insisted against my wishes on joining me in the recovery suite. As I ranted and raged at her for joining me in my supreme moment of sorrow I wondered, not for the first time, why it is that we reserve our sharpest anger for those who care about us the most.

'Now listen up, and listen well,' she said assertively, dismissing my ire.

'I've just spoken with your cardiologist. You do have a growth but in all likelihood it's benign. Your blood tests have all come back normal. And the surgeon will speak to you later this morning. He performs dozens of these operations each year. Now get a grip of yourself and stop feeling sorry for yourself.'

The amygdala, or primitive component of my brain, went berserk. 'The unadulterated cheek of her. Here I am, in the process of dying and she lectures me on feeling sorry for myself!'

Fortunately the prefrontal cortex, or conscious part of my brain, countered by saying. 'She's got a point. Relax. Don't get ahead of yourself.'

I would learn later on my journey that people who present for organ transplant and who have a stable and loving and supportive relationship have a far higher probability of surviving and thriving than those who don't. Serious illness, like serious business, thrives and responds best to positive and caring people. The antithesis is also true. I would learn in due course that I quickly needed to lose those emotional vampires who revel in the drama of your challenge and love nothing more than to regale you with their saga of doom and gloom. Frequently these people can be scarily close to you.

There was nothing negative about the medical team. They were responsive, reliable and most importantly, caring. In addition, they revered my surgeon. They left me in no doubt that not alone was he a lovely man, but that he was an outstanding surgeon and physician and acclaimed globally.

He was still draped in all his surgical regalia when he met us. Five hours of full on open heart surgery had failed to dampen an iota of his ardour and energy.

It's amazing the things that strike you about someone when you're emotionally under the cosh. I was intrigued by his accent. I couldn't quite place it. There was a clear American twang there in that he pronounced 'and' as 'end.' He'd most probably worked in the States at some stage of his career. There was also a dollop of Dublin 4 there. And I could have sworn there was a dollop of Kerry there too.

The three components of my brain – the chimp (amygdala or primitive); the champ (frontal or rational); and the computer (parietal) were engaged in open warfare. The chimp was telling me to get the hell out of there by faking a dizzy episode. The champ was advising me to stay calm; listen to the surgeon; and trust that everything would work out. The computer just kept impartially feeding me information from my vast reservoir of experiences and memories.

It reminded me that one of the best business people and most positive people I'd ever known, Lorcan Fehilly, had died from cancer of the heart.

Fortunately, it also accessed some real gems of wisdom that resonated deeply with me at that moment. In particular, I can recall vividly hearing Jim Rohn speak on wisdom:

> *Don't wish it was easier, wish you were better. Don't wish for less problems, wish for more skills. Don't wish for less challenges, wish for more wisdom.*

I heard Robin Sharma on the subject of fear:

Lean in to your fears. Go out to your edges. Because the place where your greatest limits live is also the place where your greatest growth lies.

I also clearly heard Deepak Chopra's wonderfully healing and comforting Indian accent talk of acceptance.

Today I will accept people, situations, circumstances, and events as they occur, not as how I'd like them to be.

The surgeon drew an inverted image of a heart and proceeded to scrawl in black ink what I presumed was the tumour. 'Its about a centimetre big and it's moving. It's like as if it's on a calcified stalk and it's surrounded by a circular head.'

I wondered if anything as sinister had ever been identified since TOE records began. In fact, I wondered if I'd survive the day.

Annie, sensing my despondency, interjected positively, and asked the hard question softly. 'But it's probably benign?'

I shot her a filthy look. Questions like that were designed to elicit information. More information than I wanted. Or was able to handle.

I was right. The surgeon was polite and helpful in the extreme and took full opportunity to go into detail.

'There's a good chance it's a myxoma. An atrial myxoma is a noncancerous tumour normally found on the upper left side of the heart.'

This was the kind of stuff I wanted to hear and I perked up considerably.

'But it's rare to find them on the right side. They're normally on the left.'

That fact would traumatise me for weeks to come.

'What you don't want is a carcinoma.'

I knew the chimp in my brain could produce a carcinoma in seconds so I wisely diverted that topic of conversation.

'What do you recommend I do?

'As the atrium is quite large the growth is unlikely to cause any blockage issues. However, there is always a risk of clotting. If it was on the left side that could cause a stroke. As yours is on the right, the clot would likely occur in your lung which is not as critical.'

'The challenge with this presentation is that extraction will necessitate full open heart surgery. That entails cutting through your chest muscles and breastbone and connecting you to a heart-lung bypass machine which enables me to work on your heart and extract the growth.'

'The risk for me, while present, is low. But even though you're fit and relatively young, the recovery for you will be challenging.'

'The option is that we do a PET scan and monitor the activity and the growth of the tumour over a period of time.'

It was still two days premature. But what a 53rd birthday present!

There was no need for an alarm clock the next morning.

The four pints in Linnanes had succeeded in giving me a sleeping reprieve until 3 am. Awakening came – instantly, suddenly, violently.

For some weird reason I recalled the concluding stanza of Yeats poem 'The Fisherman'.

A man who does not exist,
A man who is but a dream;
And cried, "Before I am old
I shall have written him one
Poem maybe as cold
And passionate as the dawn.

I only ever vaguely understood the references in that poem, but even as a youngish child the words, and imagery and pathos had always moved me. If they'd moved me in the past, they turbocharged me now. This was no dream. It existed. And it was as cold and passionate as the dawn.

I was terrified. There was only one thing for it. The Ultimate Worry Formula. I'd learned it from my late father-in-law who'd developed it for extreme military challenges. I had adapted the process for business scenarios and it had worked swimmingly there helping hundreds of people and organisations to practically and systematically solve their problems and worries. The question was, would it work for me?

Pat had been one of the first UN Generals to successfully bring troops in and out safely from the Congo. For twenty years, over pints on Friday evenings, I had been privileged to listen to his stories and anecdotes and humanity.

Sitting up in bed I induced a state I adapted from the teachings of Napoleon Hill and Maxwell Maltz called the 'Theatre of Your Mind.' I imagined in vivid sensory detail sitting in the pub with Pat and asking him how I could best cope with my current dilemma.

'The first thing to remember in a crisis Padraic is to remain calm. It's not sufficient just to remember to do so however, you have to programme it repeatedly deep down into your psyche. The human mind is skittish by nature and requires training. We spend years training soldiers to demand calmness of themselves in a crisis. It should be required training in every school and university in the world.'

'Command your mind to be calm. Affirm to yourself over and over that you are calm. Your mind is massively receptive to suggestion. It is programmable.'

'Secondly, there's nearly always something you can do to improve on the situation irrespective of how bad things are.' He loved relating the story of the beleaguered General who managed to send a message to Teddy Roosevelt complaining that he was hemmed in by the enemy on all sides and what could he do. Roosevelt's words were pithy and punchy.

Do what you can, with what you have, right now.

'Thirdly, you write down what you're worried about. Unemotionally, factually, objectively. It's futile doing this exercise in your head. You'll be sabotaged at every turn by your internal chatterbox. From time immemorial, at least as far back as when prehistoric man wrote on cave walls, the wise people have known the value of clarity. When you write your worries down you clarify their nature; their cause; and their power. In the army, we always maintained that a problem well defined was a problem half solved. You will be astounded at the amount of problems and worries that yield and succumb to this exercise alone. Therefore, should you ever awaken in the middle of the night and are unable to sleep, simply sit up in bed, or get up altogether and write down your worries and fears.'

'Fourthly, get the facts, and refuse absolutely to worry about the outcome until you have all the facts. It always surprises me in civilian life what critical decisions are made with insufficient or erroneous facts and information.'

'Fifth, be prepared to accept the worst if necessary. This is not necessarily a negative response. On the contrary, when we accept the worst we frequently unleash great power. Reinhold Niebuhr bestowed on us one of the greatest prayers of all time with the words:

God grant me the serenity to accept the things I cannot change; courage to change the things I can; and wisdom to know the difference.

In times of stress and anxiety, constantly repeat to yourself those words – 'serenity,' 'courage,' and 'wisdom.' Words have a deeply soothing impact on the mind.

'Sixth, improve on the worst.' I later adapted this step to include two steps. What can I do about this situation? What will I do?

'Finally Padraic, and this is most important. When you've applied all the steps of the formula, 'Let go and trust.'

'There's a power and intelligence far greater than you surging through you and around you every second of every minute of every hour of your life. You can't explain it but it exists. How else would the universe function with such miraculous ease? And this power exists to serve you. All you need do is acknowledge it, use it, trust it.'

'When you've made your decision or intention, release it to this Higher Power, and trust it absolutely, even when things don't appear to be going the way you'd planned them. Very often the outcome that materialises will be preferable to the one you intended. This is what the seers and wise people called 'faith.' Faith is believing without seeing.'

Pat used the formula in his own life many times.

Once, as a retired general, he'd been caught in a vicious fire in the MGM Hotel in Las Vegas. As other guests panicked and threw themselves from the windows Pat calmly coached the occupants on his floor to 'be calm.' He explained to them that panic and calmness were both choices. He then outlined certain facts about their present situation. Sure, there was a fire, and a serious fire. As of yet, however, there were no visible flames; the fire services were at the scene in profusion; and the structure of the rooms was built of the finest fireproof materials. In addition, he made them aware of the fact that most mortalities in fires arise from smoke inhalation rather than burning. Collectively, they made the decision to remain in their rooms as opposed to randomly running down the smoke-filled fire escapes or worse still, jumping to an inevitable death. Crucially, they began to wet duvets and sheets in the baths and line the doors and windows to prevent smoke inhalation. And, they trusted in a Higher Power.

After one hour they were rescued by the fire services, who provided them with oxygen masks and escorted them in 'blind darkness' down several stories of fire escapes.

Like Pat in the MGM Hotel, I too was on fire. There may yet be no visible flames but there was certainly smoke. The issue was, how could I get through the weekend without cracking up?

The answer seemed to be 'The Ultimate Worry Formula.'

At 4:25 am on Saturday May 31st I sat up in bed and tackled the first step in the formula – be calm. How can you conceivably be calm when you're mind is like a paddock of wild horses on a stampede?

Fortunately I had a strategy for calmness. For twenty five years I've meditated reasonably consistently. I first learned TM – Transcendental Meditation – and then graduated to a hybrid of yoga postures and breathing. For the past decade I've cheated. I use a binaural recording that induces deep alpha and theta brain activity for an hour most mornings.

I meditated now. And it did calm me.

At 5.30 am I did a 'Teddy Roosevelt.' I asked myself what 'I could do, with what I had, right now.'

The answer was to get out of bed, stop moping and feeling sorry for myself and systematically tackle 'The Ultimate Worry Formula.'

I opened the iPad and wrote down in bold type.

WHAT AM I WORRIED ABOUT?

I'm worried I'm going to die soon and in great suffering and I'm scared out of my wits.

WHAT ARE THE FACTS?

Negative. Irrefutable evidence of a growth in my heart.

Positive. Good angiogram. Perfect head MRI. Normal blood tests.

WHAT'S THE WORST THAT CAN HAPPEN?

I'll die soon, in agony.

CAN I ACCEPT THAT?

With great difficulty. But if I have to, I have to. We all will go sometime.

WHAT CAN I DO ABOUT IT?

1. Nothing. Hope it goes away.
2. Kill myself.
3. Ring the Blackrock Clinic on Tuesday and confirm the results of the other two cat scans. If they're clear, that's fantastic. If not, that's another issue and I'll deal with it then.
4. Joseph Campbell said that 'The cave you fear to enter holds your greatest treasure.' Be prepared to take

every diagnostic test and scan the medics prescribe to get the facts.

5. And take Dale Carnegie's advice. 'Live your life in daylight compartments' and don't worry about the results until Tuesday.

6. Get the growth extracted as quickly as possible – next two weeks – and determine exactly what it is.

7. Get around really positive and uplifting people who have whacked problems like this. Learn what their mindset was?

8. Have a positive expectancy.

WHAT WILL I DO ABOUT IT?

1. I'll ring the Clinic first thing on Tuesday morning - it was a bank holiday weekend - and get the results of the scans and refuse to faff about it over the weekend.

2. I'll continue to meditate every day.

3. I'll exercise like an athlete every day.

4. I'll 'run as far as I can see' and avoid getting ahead of myself.

5. I'll meet my accountant on Tuesday and plan the financial implications of taking three months out of work.

6. I'll get brilliant hypnosis on healing.

7. I'll affirm 1000 times a day that I AM IN PERFECT HEALTH – whether I believe it or not.

8. I will create an awesome motivational training programme with the real credibility of having been through a crisis.

9. I'll get around some really uplifting people such as Liam Ryan, David Tarpey, Sister Colette and Pat Harry.
10. I'll make an appointment with Larry McMahon and do some deep healing work on my thinking.
11. I'll take great supplements and alkalise my body.
12. I'll manage the wild ponies.
13. I'll resolve to live as much as possible in the present moment choosing neither to dwell on the past or in the future as both are illusions.
14. I'll refuse to feel sorry for myself realising that right now, someone, somewhere is worse off than me.

I can't say I was jumping around the garden having completing the exercise but it had provided more clarity, more focus and at least, there was a semblance of a plan there.

Although still only 6 am, I slipped on my skins and my runners and I jogged out gingerly along the Flaggy Shore. It was as if Heaney had written PostScript solely for me.

> And some time make the time to drive out west
> Into County Clare, along the Flaggy Shore,
> You are neither here nor there,
> A hurry through which known and strange things pass
> As big soft buffetings come at the car sideways
> And catch the heart off guard and blow it open.

The dawn didn't appear quite as cold.

Chapter 5
Routine Matters

I remember my late mother saying that the only difference between surgery in the old days and today is that today the knives are sharper.

Joe Connolly. All Ireland Winning Captain.

It never occurred to me that I might die during the operation the following morning.

More precisely, I refused to allow it occur to me.

My wife and three sons were piled tight into Room 419 of the Blackrock Clinic and tonight, of all nights, I needed to show leadership. There would be no room for self-pity or self-doubt.

Whatever wild horses I would entertain in the small wee hours of the morning would be securely bridled until then. For better or worse, I'd mastered this thought management strategy at boarding school where it was considered more advantageous to reserve displays of sorrow and pity for the privacy of the dormitory rather than to lavishly brandish them in public.

And it worked, for the most part.

On the surface, the craic was great. My wife distributed amusing vignettes from the family archives like a well-tuned scrum half and the three lads ran clever lines of running on to stories that for the most part featured themselves positively. It greatly confused the visitors in the corridor outside. The humour inherent in imminent open heart surgery the next morning was for the most part lost on them.

The fun abated abruptly with the arrival of the surgeon at 10 pm.

I'd been told he'd been performing a heart transplant on a child that afternoon and he mightn't get to see me that night. All evening I'd willed that to be the case.

The lads awkwardly shuffled up to make room for him. It was ironic to see three big handsome lads divest their power to another person. For all their young lives they had held their Dad's heart in their hands. Tomorrow, another man would also.

I protested to the surgeon that it was late in the evening and that he had far better things than to be doing than discussing my upcoming operation. I informed him that I had total confidence in his ability and I was a staunch supporter of the mantra that 'where ignorance is bliss 'tis folly to be wise.'

He wasn't wearing it. I marvelled at the sheer stamina and fortitude of the man. Despite a harrowing day over an operating table in a sterile theatre giving life to a little girl, he still retained perfect composure and proceeded to go through tomorrow's process in detail. Minute detail.

'We will enter the chest cavity via an eight inch incision and then saw through the sternum or breast bone. We will then connect you to a heart-lung machine. This machine temporarily takes over the heart's job of pumping oxygen-rich blood to the organs and tissues enabling me to operate on your heart.'

Most of the detail flowed off me like water off the proverbial ducks back. It's said that in times of trauma one only processes a fraction of the detail or content being described. What I did process though was the shock and revulsion on the faces and demeanours of Annie and the kids.

Sensing my distraction, he proceeded once again to revert to the ubiquitous diagram. Taking my Smácht folder pad from my bedside locker, he proceeded to sketch out my heart in large detail. On the right atrium, he scribbled in the nodule like a kid drawing with crayons. I can assure you I processed that. It was big and black and foreboding.

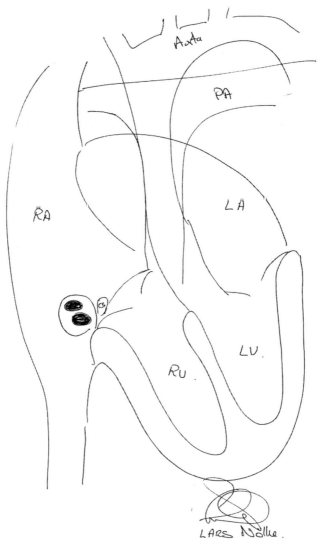

This is the diagram sketched by Lars Nolke on that infamous day in my life, July 10th 2014, depicting what the growth looked like and where it was situated. (He kindly signed it for me later.)

'Depending on what the growth is I have a number of options. If it's a myxoma, I simply cut it out and stitch back the heart lining. If it's cancerous I may need to be more aggressive and take some tissue from around the growth. If I inadvertently interfere with the electrical circuit in your heart, which is invisible, I will have to insert a pacemaker. Anything I remove will be sent for histology in the laboratory.'

'Any questions?'

I flashed a scowl that would have stopped Jonah Lomu dead in his tracks that there would be no questions.

I couldn't believe the response. No one obeyed. Like a great teacher, expounding on their specialist subject, the surgeon had my assembled family riveted and stimulated. Shane was first in.

'How long will it take to get a reply from the lab on the histology?

Although he's now much bigger and fitter than me, I'd still have clocked him in the ear if I could have got close to him.

'Between five and ten working days,' replied the surgeon helpfully.

The floodgates opened. They all wanted in on the quiz show.

'How long will you have his heart in your hands?

'What happens if it doesn't start beating when you put it back?

'What happens if the stitches come loose?

Harry, a Law student, bided his time and asked the quintessential bitch of a question.

'What other risks are there that we mightn't have considered?'

'Good question Harry. There's the risk of a stroke. There's the risk of a clot. If that happened on the left side it's likely to lodge in the brain. It's less serious on the right side however as it would clot in the lungs.'

His patience and perseverance in fielding and dealing thoroughly with each question spoke volumes about his attention to detail. Despite the discomfort of having to sit through the hard questions I felt assured and confident that I was in the hands of a master. I was giving myself every opportunity. I trusted.

I think anaesthesia should rank as one of the Wonders of the World. Imagine being sawn open and worked on for a period of four hours without feeling nada.

I came to in the Intensive Care Unit at about 10 pm that Friday evening. Same audience. Different vibration. Annie and the kids all told me I'd done great. The cynic in me knew that they'd say this irrespective of the outcome.

From some recess of my being, I managed to address the surgeon through the drugs and the duskiness.

'Was it a myxoma?' (Myxoma being a benign and harmless tumour.)

'No. It looks like a cyst that had become calcified and it looks as if it has been there for a very, very long time, and I got it all out. It's gone off to the lab now for the histology, so for now, ignore it.'

I was devastated. For the past three weeks, I had visualised intensively that the outcome would have been a harmless myxoma. I became suspicious that the surgeon was sugar coating the news.

A male nurse gave me a tablet. When I asked him what it was, he replied in his finest Dublin brogue. 'If I had a few of them out in the street there I'd get a fair few quid for them.' I learned later that it was an opiate and is used to relax and relieve pain. Like the anaesthetic, it worked perfectly. Saturday arrived. My stats were good and I was back in a private suite overlooking hundreds of kids learning to sail Mirror dinghies on Dublin Bay.

The morphine had failed to suppress the overpowering feeling that I may have cancer. I realised I was back on the dance floor with wild horses. If I failed to control them, they'd inexorably run amok. What the morphine failed to do in terms of emotion it compensated for by way of a surge in creativity.

As if possessed by an invisible force for good I began to doodle on my Smácht folder pad.

POM = (F + 3As) × S

Peace of Mind = (Focus + Attitude + Associations + Actions) ×
Smácht

I'd been warned that open heart surgery could induce a myriad of emotions. I'd assumed these were of the negative variety. On the contrary, I was now being assailed by the most peaceful of feelings. For the first time in weeks, if not months, I experienced total peace of mind.

I became heedless to the outcome of the histology. I let go on the plethora of worries that had been assailing me like how my business would survive if I'm out of work for a protracted period of time. I released utterly. Vast reservoirs of pent up stress literally subsided from my being.

It struck me that 'peace of mind' should be my ultimate objective.

'But peace of mind is an illusion; a fantasy; an escapism from reality,' I heard a wild horse say in my head. 'How could you, such an inveterate worrier, ever achieve peace of mind, and particularly with you hooked up to so many tubes and intravenous devices!'

If I'd learned one thing on this current journey, it was to facilitate a balanced discussion between my 'wild horses' (or chimp) and my 'guardian angels' (or champ).

'Peace of mind' is a function of five separate yet connected forces,' replied the champ.

1. Focus

You can either live your dreams or you can live your fears.

Les Brown

This quote states categorically that what we focus on multiplies.

Every second of every minute of every hour, we have a choice – to choose what we focus on.

I realised in that instant, that despite all the tubes attached to me, I now had a choice. I could choose to focus on getting sick or getting healed. The outcome would depend on my choice of focus.

2. Attitude

There is little difference in people. That little difference is attitude. The big difference is whether that attitude is positive or negative.

Og Mandinho

I encountered it every step along this journey. I witnessed the sickest of people with little or no formal education light up entire hospital wards – with their attitude. By the same token, I observed many eminently qualified people suck the lifeblood from those in their company – with their attitude. I recall one jovial bedfellow of mine comment on a dreary consultant as being 'One of the rare few who can light up a room, by his departure.'

Attitude is the fire beneath your focus. It too is a choice.

3. Associations

> *You are the average of the five people you're surrounded by most of the time.*

> Jim Rohn

I'll tell you about the power of associations.

Last Thursday, October 22nd, my first association of the day was at 8.30 am with my consultant. He has the most magnificent mind for detail and facts. Regrettably, his detail of the facts relating to my health were not positive. My CRP (infection and inflammation) levels were elevated. My renal function was under pressure and my blood pressure was up. That discussion, whilst absolutely necessary, propelled me into a downer for the morning.

The bottom line is that different 'associations' affect your 'peace of mind' massively.

I learned to find a space in my mind where I could meet with and associate only with those who made me feel better.

4. Actions

Actions speak louder than words.

When you think about it some of the most peaceful people in the world took great action. Think of people like Nelson Mandella, Mother Teresa, Gandhi, John Hume. These were people who became fulfilled by immersing themselves in massive action.

I once heard the late Fr. Michael Cleary asked how he responded when he got news that he had throat cancer. His reply was that he'd gotten into his car and 'drove 150 miles to play in a Goal charity match in Mayo.' He went on to elaborate that his strategy for coping was to immerse himself in action and keep busy. Some might query the nature of his actions but there's no denying that his 'activity' resulted in him living way in advance of his medical prognosis.

5. Smácht

Attitude gets you moving. Smácht keeps you going.

I have an aversion to the word 'discipline.'

I was weaned by my teachers, my mother and the Catholic Church that 'discipline' was the stuff of character and a quality that I was singularly lacking in it. It became a self-fulfilling prophesy. My reports from school repeatedly reported that I had 'poor discipline.' My mother despaired and berated me for this. The priests preached to me about disciplining myself against 'impure thoughts.' Imagine telling that to a young teenager in boarding school for eight weeks at a trot! It was tantamount to telling the tide not to come in on Lahinch Beach on a Spring tide.

But intuitively, I knew that discipline worked. The results spoke for themselves. Every great occasion in my life was preceded by discipline. Moving from the 'C' class to the 'B' class and finally, the 'A' class was all achieved through discipline, whereas most regrets in my young life pivoted around a lack of discipline. Failure to get on the senior rugby team was as much a function of a lack of focused discipline than innate talent. Why, even successfully chatting up girls was as much a function of a disciplined approach as looks or charm!

If only discipline wasn't synonymous with hard work and abstinence and punishment!

In 1979, I was a member of the first non-Gaeltacht school ever to win the Gael Linn Munster Debating Championship. We won six successive debates in a row. At the time it was considered something of a coup and even succeeded in featuring in some of the 'Dublin media.' I recall my mother lamentably commenting that if I'd displayed a fraction of the discipline I'd had towards debating to other areas of my life that I could have amounted to something.

And then the penny dropped. I had what trendy coaches refer to as a 'paradigm shift' in my thinking.

We never regarded ourselves as disciplined or hard working or put upon on that debating team. We did it because we:

- Loved it (passion)
- Were rewarded (approval, achievement, recognition, a couple of pints each time we won), but mostly, we
- BECAME ADDICTED TO THE ROUTINE

Each week for six weeks the routine was exactly the same. We'd get a general motion on the Tuesday to be debated the following Monday. We began to crave the receipt of that motion. That evening we'd sit down with Brendan O'Rourke, our trainer, and mind-map responses to that motion. Then we'd practice. Over and over again. It wasn't work. We actually enjoyed 'the practice of practice.' We craved the routine, the reward and the rush.

The Munster Final was against Coláiste Íde from Dingle in the neutral venue of Laurel Hill Convent in Limerick. The analogy was made that it was similar to Tipperary playing Kerry in football. No one gave us a chance. They were native speakers; had won it more than any other school in the past; and as my mother would testify, I had no track record with the motion.

The motion was 'Smácht.' The Irish word for 'discipline.'

'Discipline' is the master key to all progress in life. Every baby that's ever walked has known that. They have oodles of inbuilt 'discipline' programmed into every cell in their bodies. It never occurs to them to give up each and every time they fall as they first attempt to walk. They just get on with it enjoying the routine of practice.

The paradox of Smácht is that if you make what you love doing your burning passion, you'll never actually have to use Smácht. It'll occur naturally.

Chapter 6
Put Brain in Motion before Moving Anything

I always had a soft spot for physiotherapists.

My Auntie Mary, quite the kindest, wisest and coolest person you'd ever encounter, was a physiotherapist and lived with us until I was eight years old.

As a kid, the Physio Department in the Regional Hospital in Galway was the ultimate adventure centre for a young kid. On rare occasions, when Mary would have been delayed with a patient and I'd be left waiting in reception, I'd skive off in and try out the equipment.

There were bikes and treadmills there with real speedometers like you only ever saw on TV. There were muscle-building machines like those displayed on ads in comics for Charles Atlas. There were climbing frames to shimmy up and over. And there was this weird machine that once made my left arm go completely red. It also made Mary, the most peaceful of ladies, go bright red when she discovered I'd successfully self-administered the ultraviolet machine. How the modern child's potential for adventure has been thwarted by those people from 'Health and Safety'!

As a student, I'd gotten to see a completely different side to physiotherapists. The Physio girls – there were only girls doing it in those days – were unanimously acknowledged as the best looking and most attractive students in UCD. I'd hit it lucky and gotten invited to their annual dress dance in the Gresham. This was no ordinary 'Dinner Dance.' This was a parade; a performance; a spectacle. As I sat people watching and marvelling at their beauty and appeal, a great friend of mine from my Roscrea days followed my thoughts.

'It's something about the way they move,' he explained, neatly paraphrasing George Harrison.

'What do you mean?

'Carriage. Deportment. Posture. They get it. They teach the stuff. Observe them. They're always moving with elegance, élan and grace. Why, even when they're sitting they're moving.'

I never realised, however, what physios actually do until after my operation.

It's strange, but I could tell she was a physio by the way she entered the room. Even though I'd been asleep, and this was only my first morning back in the ward, I'd already begun to recognise the presence of the different people entering the room. Consultants arrive with authority. You hear them coming well in advance from outside on the corridor amidst a clamour of noise, commotion and kerfuffle. Nurses enter efficiently and on purpose. They're almost always doing a job as they enter. Physios however, appear with stealth. They're there before you realise it. It's that deportment thing again.

And there was also the smell giveaway. Most obvious were my great friends – the catering people. There is no more welcoming and edifying aroma than that of tea and toast no matter how sick you are. Not so the phlebotomists. I could always sense their presence by the acrid smell of strong disinfectant and chlorine. Physios however, are instantly recognisable by the scent of hand lotion. An earthy, grounded and invigorating blend of basil, cedar wood and lime. How many times had I witnessed my Auntie Mary applying liberal dollops of hand lotion to her hands and then proceeding to vigorously rub it in – even as she was driving!

'Good morning Padraic,' she said cheerfully. 'My name's Julie and my job is to have you walking like a trooper in jig time.'

'When were you planning on that? I asked smugly, and still half asleep.

'No time like the present.'

'Julie, I don't know if you're aware,' I replied, rapidly coming to.

'I'm only just after surgery. I feel as if I was run over by a lorry. And what's more, I'm hooked to a plethora of intravenous devices.'

'I've a pretty good idea how you feel Pádraic. You feel as if you've a brick lying on your chest. You're absolutely exhausted. And you'd much prefer to stay in bed and hope that I disappear 'til another day.'

'I've been a Chartered Physiotherapist for ten years now and I've helped hundreds of people, many much worse than you, to be walking confidently before they go home. If you're interested in getting out as early as next Wednesday, then walking with me, is the quickest way to doing that.'

I'd taught sales training to the good and great and our Julie was right on up there with the best of them. She'd hit all the criteria – empathy; assurance; evidence that she could get results; and crucially, motivation to get me to take action.

Reinforcing the latter, she continued.

'In addition to getting out as early as Wednesday of next week there are three other good reasons to get walking as soon as possible.

It will exercise your heart muscle which will give you more energy and make you feel less tired.
It will exercise all of the other muscles in your body which means you'll be more flexible and have less pain.
It will exercise your mind muscle which will make you feel better and lift your spirits.

Mentally, I was now wide awake and raring to go. Physically however, I couldn't move an inch without considerable pain and distress.

'Julie, the doctors have warned me that my severed breast bone is just connected by a few strands of wire and that I can't lift anything over two pounds weight. How am I ever going to haul my body out of the bed let alone stand up and walk?'

'Pádraic, the doctors are technically right and you need to be extremely careful how you move. I'm here however to tell you what you can do, and the first thing you can do is to put your brain in motion before moving your body. Write that down please.'

I'd later christen it 'Julie's First Jewel.'

'Put Brain in Motion Before Moving Body.'

'In order to be able to get out of bed there are only three things you need to remember. I want you to write these down in your notebook also so you won't forget.'

'Hands across chest. Use tummy muscles. Shuffle on bum.'

That mantra would become my best friend over the next six weeks. It worked. I was now sitting on the side of the bed.

'Our goal today is to walk one side of the cardiology block – a distance of 30 yards – in under ten minutes.'

I thought back just three weeks to our great Smáchter Frank Byrnes. Frank had run 100 kilometres over a ten and a half hour period. I had joined him for one 5K circuit of running through Portumna Woods. It wasn't earth shattering stuff, but I'd done it. And now I was being asked to walk a mere 30 yards and I feared I couldn't do it. Weakly, I succumbed to my fears. Then I gave them authority.

'I can't do it,' I blurted out lazily and without thinking.

'That's the next mindset we're going to change. Repeat after me three times.'

- 'Put Brain in Motion Before Moving Mouth'.
- I can walk 30 yards.
- I will walk 30 yards.
- I am walking 30 yards.

'Now I'm going out for a few minutes. I want you to close your eyes and quieten your mind. When it's perfectly still, I want you to picture yourself walking those 30 yards – steadily, strongly and soundly.'

When she returned she attached my various accoutrements to a mobile stand, and supporting me by the arm, we commenced my marathon of 30 yards. For something I'd done thoughtlessly for 50 odd years it seemed mightily incongruous to be making such a song and dance about walking now. After a few paces I stumbled on the corridor. The pain was quite severe and again, without thinking, I protested that 'I can't do it.'

'Repeat after me three times.

- 'Put Brain In Motion Before Moving Mouth;.
- I can walk 30 yards.
- I will walk 30 yards.
- I am walking 30 yards.'

It sounded stupid but it distracted my wild horses, encouraged my reserves of strength and provided me with tangible, albeit slow evidence that I was walking – progressing.

When we returned to my room Julie asked me to write down in my Smácht folder.

'I walked 30 yards in ten minutes.' Pádraic Ó Máille. July 13th 2014.

They were the slowest 30 yards I'd ever walked in my adult life but they were the quickest lessons I'd ever received on the laws of success. The following day, with Julie's help I walked two sides of the cardiology ward – 60 yards. The next day, Tuesday, I completed a whole circuit – 120 yards all on my own. On Wednesday I was discharged. And that Friday I walked the Flaggy Shore in County Clare.

Sometime on that Sunday afternoon a beautiful bouquet of uplifting sunflowers arrived addressed to me. They were from Annie's goddaughter Laura – another physio – all the way from New Zealand.

I understood for the first time in my life what physios the world over really do. They help people feel better about themselves.

WHAT I LEARNED FROM JULIE

1. **Find a therapist who'll show you what you can do and dismiss with abandon those, therapists or other, who persist in telling you what you can't do.** Apply this to every sphere of your life. Choose to live your life around 'can do' people and jettison the rest.

2. **Put brain in motion before moving body**. Many people begin their day like busy fools. Having pressed the snooze button once too often they realise with horror that they're already late before they even start. This precipitates a cycle of disorder, disorganisation and distress that culminates in exhaustion and inefficiency. It doesn't have to be this way. Take a few minutes to engage your mind before exhausting your body. The motivational writer Steve Pavlina once said 'The first hour is the rudder of the day. If I'm lazy or haphazard in my actions during the first hour after I wake up, I tend to have a fairly lazy and unproductive day. But if I strive to make that first hour optimally productive, the rest of the day tends to follow suit.'

What a wonderful expression and metaphor! Emblazon that image indelibly on your mind. 'The first hour is the rudder of my day.' Sadly, so many people press that snooze button on their most productive lever of the day. Like so many other jewels of wisdom in this book, how you use your mornings is ultimately your choice. Imagine if you could duplicate the success Julie had with me in getting me out of bed and having me walk again? You can. The following six routines are all that you'll ever need to guarantee unparalleled success in every area of your life. They are synthesised from the exact process she used and are now being used with massive success by Smáchters everywhere. They can be completed in as little as six minutes so now you have no excuses for turbo-charging your results.

3. **Start every day for the rest of your life with a great SHAG.** I don't care who you're sleeping beside, make no apologies about starting the day with a great SHAG.

A SHAG is a first cousin of the world famous acronym BHAG which stands for Big Hairy Audacious Goal except that SHAG stands for Smácht Hairy Accountable Goal. There are four components to a great SHAG.

Firstly, working backwards on the word, goals are critical to your success in life. Zig Ziglar famously said that 'Success is goals. Everything else is just commentary.' Many people, when they eventually do struggle to get out of bed, simply start doing without thinking. As we constantly reiterate in Smácht. 'There's no point going faster if you're going in the wrong direction.'

Secondly, you need to be <u>accountable</u> to the pursuit of your goals. What's gets measured gets done so either measure your progress yourself or find someone else who'll do it for you.

Thirdly your goal needs to be hairy or humungous. Impotent goals beget impotent results. Dream big. Fourthly, despite what Rhonda Byrne in *The Secret* said, goals are insufficient by themselves. They need to be preceded by Smácht. No goal, however wimpish or audacious, was ever achieved without Smácht. Your first task therefore is to begin every day with a great SHAG. It's futile having a great SHAG tomorrow and forgetting about it until you end up in trouble again. SHAGGING is neither an ad hoc, à la carte or casual approach to life. Rather, it's a committed, structured and process-driven philosophy for achieving great results in every area of your life. Julie's SHAG for me on that first morning was 'to walk one side of the cardiology block – a distance of 30 yards – in under ten minutes.'

4. **Put brain in motion before moving mouth**. Like it or not, you are engaged in one never-ending internal dialogue. Even when you're asleep you're talking to yourself through your dreams. And like it or not, you're subconscious mind is constantly responding to this dialogue. For many, their internal dialogue begins when the alarm goes off. One part of your mind – the logical or conscious mind – says, 'it's time to get up. You have an important appointment at 8.30.' But then, another part of your mind – the infinitely more powerful subconscious mind – taunts

you with, 'it's freezing cold outside and it's so cosy and snug and warm beneath the duvet. Stay on for just another ten minutes.' And so the conversation proceeds – for your day, for your week, for your life.

But you always have choices. You can control the conversation in your mind. It's called 'Affirmation.' Few people espoused and practiced the law of affirmation more successfully than Mohammed Ali. In an interview with Michael Parkinson he revealed that 'I said 'I was the greatest' long before I ever was the greatest.' This is tantamount to faking it before making it and is based on a well known neurological fact – that the subconscious mind is incapable of distinguishing between what is real and imagined.

Furthermore, the words 'I am' are two of the most creative words in the universe. The reality is that subconsciously you are using them all the time. 'I am' are the two words that most frequently underpin and fuel your belief system. How often have you undermined yourself by repeating ad nausea to yourself – 'I am useless at maths or English or computers; 'I am no good at football or athletics or hockey; I am not destined to make it as a business person/parent/lover. The great news is that you can supplant those negative and disempowering belief systems with an infinite array of positive sequences such as 'I am attractive', 'I am beautiful', 'I am courageous', 'I am decisive', 'I am enthusiastic', 'I am the funniest person in the room', 'I am healthy as a trout'.

An 'I am' affirmation that I found particularly useful when I found myself in health trouble was the affirmation 'I am responsible.' Brian Tracy states that 'in every situation, the antidote to negative emotions is to say, "I am responsible". The mark of the leader, the truly superior person, is that he or she accepts complete responsibility for the situation.'

5. **'Be still and know that I am God.'** This is taken from the bible and is the first prayer you need when you find yourself in times of trouble. If you have issues with the word 'God', simply drop it and it works just as well. The key benefit is in stilling the mind and body. There is real power in being still. Let's call it Still Power. The great Austrian poet Frank Kafka explains how to achieve Still Power. 'You do not need to leave your room. Remain sitting at your table and listen. Do not even listen, simply wait, be quiet still and solitary. The world will freely offer itself to you to be unmasked, it has no choice, it will roll in ecstasy at your feet.' You guys in Smácht don't even need to leave your bed.

6. **Record your victories**. By far and away, the Smácht exercise that has consistently received the greatest feedback since we started the programme is 'Smácht Victories.' Very simply, participants describe their victories since we last met. Typical victories are simple things like 'I ran three miles'; 'I took my family away on a holiday'; 'I remained off the booze for three whole weeks and I loved it'; 'I thrashed out a business plan that really excites me'; 'I fired an employee who did nothing but dampen morale

and cause me emotional and financial trouble for years and I can't tell you the relief of it.' The cynics will argue that we're cherry picking and promoting a Pollyanna approach to business and life. My response is that if it makes you feel better, so what!

7. **Lists work. List your actions. Then JFDT. (Just Fricking Do Them).** You wouldn't want to go to a meeting without an agenda. The same holds for your day. Having a list may not ensure you will get everything done everyday but as that erudite teacher Sybil F. Partridge declared back in 1925. 'Just for today I will have a program. I may not follow it exactly, but I will have it. I will save myself from two pests: hurry and indecision.'

8. **'Motion creates emotion.' Get moving.** Sir Isaac Newton, the most eminent scientist of his day, proved in his First Law of Motion that 'An object at rest stays at rest and an object in motion stays in motion with the same speed and in the same direction unless acted upon by an unbalanced force.' That means that if you're feeling miserable and you do nothing about it, you're guaranteed to remain that way. Go for a walk, however, and you'll feel better. Go for a run and you'll feel better again. Go for a swim in the sea and you'll feel unstoppable.

As we explained earlier, good routines precede good habits. And good habits are what makes life liveable. In fact, your entire persona craves routine. In order therefore to change your results, whether you're in trouble or not, change your routines. The best routine, the rudder of your day, is to start your day with 'Julie's Jewels.' Before you get out of bed in the morning take just six minutes to SASVAM:

1. SHAG
2. Affirm
3. StillPower
4. **Victorise**
5. Act
6. Move

Chapter 7
Control the Controllables

Over the years I'd become all too familiar with the fear of waiting for the phone to ring. I'd won and lost a myriad of lucrative contracts over the phone. I'd been dumped, ditched and propositioned over the phone.

I received my Leaving Cert results in the only public telephone kiosk on Inis Mór on the Aran Islands. I had to coerce a slew of islanders to patiently desist from making a call themselves in order to free up the incoming line. I can't remember my greater fear – the intensifying wrath of the locals or the results themselves.

When eventually the phone call did come, the reception and the results held out good until Fr. Peter got to my maths result, my bête noir. All my other results would count for nought if I failed maths. Regrettably, his delivery of my maths result coincided with a blast of hissy static from the radio of the incoming LE Naomh Eanna. I couldn't quite distinguish from his voice whether I'd gotten an 'E' or a 'D'. My future career teetered precariously on that outcome.

'Was it a 'D' or an 'E,' I implored timidly.

'D' for 'Donald Duck,' he roared above the interference.

As I punched the air in triumph I couldn't help but over-hear the conversation behind me.

'Cén chaoi ar eirigh leis? (How did he get on?) asked an elderly man in báinín's and bréidíns at the rear of the queue.

'Níl a fhios agam go díreach, ach fuair sé Donald Duck san sums,' (I don't know exactly, but he got a Donald Duck in sums) replied the lady to the front who'd by now suc-ceeded in getting her ear almost as close to the receiver as mine.

'Is léir go bhfuil Ollamh in ár lár,' (it seems we have a Pro-fessor in our midst) said the old man with more than a snatch of sarcasm.

I awoke the morning following my discharge from hospi-tal dreading the ringing of the phone. My surgeon had re-assured me that he'd phone me the moment he got my histology results but that that could be as many as ten working days. I'd somehow convinced myself that he was managing my expectations and that I'd hear from him sooner rather than later.

Each time the phone rang my recently reengineered heart missed a beat. And the phone never stopped ringing. Dozens of genuine and warm well wishers, learning that I was home, called to express their good wishes. I quietly extolled the virtues of caller ID.

By lunchtime that Thursday I was mentally and physically exhausted.

I rehearsed a myriad of different scenarios in my mind.

I thought of Jim Mitchell, the former Fine Gael Minister for Communications, who, following tests, had received a phone call from his doctor at 9.20 one morning. The phone call was abrupt, to the point and devoid of any small talk. Jim was told he had cancer of the liver and it was inoperable.

To his eternal credit and courage, he succeeded in corralling that news to a secure part of his mind and proceeded to chair a five-hour long meeting of a Tribunal hearing in the full glare of the media and the public. It was only then that he called his wife and broke the news to her.

That was grace under pressure. Joey the clown would have applauded his ability to keep his head under the most extreme pressure and still keep the show on the road.

I was by no means as composed. By 3 pm that afternoon I capitulated beneath the fear of that anticipated call and diverted my phone to the airplane feature which disables any calls from being received. It was a temporary respite that was more than penalised for when I had to endure the terror of seeing what calls I had missed.

To my credit, I'd managed the ordeal of the operation with reasonable aplomb. To be fair, the team ensured that at all times things were under control – 'faoi Smácht.' Moreover, I trusted implicitly that if things did take a turn for the worse that this team had the experience, expertise and nous to solve almost any issue.

Waiting for the phone to ring with a result that could go either way was, however, largely outside my control – gan Smácht. My amygdala or primitive mind was in a tailspin.

It would be in the dead of the following night before I succeeded in quelling the clamour of wild horses in my head. My father had an expression that 'too far East is West' and that's exactly what happened. My mind finally tired of being frightened and terrified and I was visited by a sensation of peace and of tranquillity and of insight.

In fact, I gave up being frightened. I surrendered. I handed the result of that phone call and all it's implications completely over to a Higher Power.

The release of that pent up tension induced in me the deepest of deep sleeps and I awoke the following morning with a semblance of a plan. I resolved to take control of certain aspects of the day that I could control. I made a deal with the twin components of my mind – the amygdala or irrational mind, and the prefrontal cortex, the rational mind – that I would sweat over answering the phone today, but only on my terms. I would divert the phone all day except between 12 noon and 1 pm and 5 pm and 6 pm. In that way I was neither avoiding the call indefinitely nor sweating about it incessantly.

In the meantime, I would occupy my mind and body as actively as I could this day. That morning, just one week after surgery I walked the Flaggy Shore. At least I walked the west-east aspect of it with a force four firmly in my back. There'd be plenty enough time to face into the wind when I became stronger.

That afternoon I observed Noel and PJ McInerney build a stone wall the way stone walls have been built since time immemorial. They worked stone as tastily as my surgeon had worked heart tissue the previous Friday. All three were masters of their craft. They trusted in results without rushing the process. I would too.

That evening I tested the parameters of my strength to the limit. For the first six weeks after the operation I was under the strictest of instructions to lift no more than two kilograms of weight. Imagine my delight therefore when discovering that a pint of Guinness weighs exactly two kilograms, and that the quicker I imbibed it, the lighter it got. Happy days!

The phone call didn't come until the following Wednesday afternoon. And when it did, I missed it.

The 'Missed Calls' feature on my mobile phone had captured it however. There it was in bright blood red. 'The Blackrock Clinic.' And another little bright blood red circle beside the phone icon on my landing page indicated there was a message awaiting me in my voice mail.

For the umpteenth time since this health travail had started my mind went into overdrive. Both the amygdala and prefrontal cortex knew full well that this was no message from 'Housekeeping' informing me that they'd retrieved my lost stripy sock from the washing machine. This message would define my future like no other message I'd ever received.

The amygdala appeared in all it's '3F' Glory beseeching me to 'Freeze or Flee or Fight.' And for an instant I did freeze. I actually had deluded myself into believing that this phone call would never come and that the entire event had been one big bad dream. That thought was rapidly interrupted by a more appealing one which was to flee to the pub and pretend that the message wasn't there at all. I have to concede, it had it's merits.

And then, from some recess of my infinite subconscious mind came a vignette that my Uncle Stíofáin had shared with me as a kid. Each year he'd visit his brother in America and together they'd explore and hunt the vast plains and mountains of that massive nation. This particular year they'd been to Colorado and he explained to me that this is one of the few places in the world where cattle and buffalo roam together. He described to me the similarities between these two animals and yet how one is much more intelligent than the other.

'When a storm approaches, both animals can sense it in their being but are programmed to respond to it differently. The cattle, knowing that the prevailing winds come from the west instinctively head east, in order to outrun the storm. But as you know, cattle are slow and awkward and are rapidly overhauled by the speed of the storm. And instead of actually outrunning the storm, they simply end up running with it.

'The buffalo on the other hand, wait until the storm is at it's height, and then proceed to charge head on in to it. To be sure, it's difficult and frightening to begin with, but very quickly they emerge the far side of the storm. They sensibly end up minimising their exposure to it.

'And so it is with people. Many flee their problems hoping to avoid the pain and suffering involved in confronting them. In so doing they ironically maximise their exposure to misery and hardship.

'Clever people however, realise that problems are part and parcel of life, and that the quicker and harder they charge at them, the quicker they are resolved and overcome.

'Pádraiceen, you may think a time will come when all is rosy and you'll be problem free. The reality is that you'll always have problems. And while this sounds negative, it doesn't have to be. The day you realise that charging head on at your greatest challenges is the day you become free, because that's the day you realise you have the solution to overcoming all your cares and worries.'

He would never know it, but 45 years after he told it, that story would be the tipping point for me in determining whether I fought or fled on the field of possibly my greatest challenge.

I dialled the number. The accent was unmistakeable. You could have buried half of west coast America, south Dublin and mid-Kerry into it's cadences and inflections. The tonality however was actor perfect neutral. It betrayed not a scintilla of evidence as to whether the news it was about to deliver was positive or negative.

The words did that. I replayed them over and over again.

'Pádraic, the results are very, very good. The preliminary histology reveals a calcified cyst which as I suspected was there a very, very long time. It's totally benign and there's nothing sinister to report. A detailed report will follow in the next fortnight.'

You'd think that after two full months of protracted apprehension and anxiety that the floodgates of unbridled euphoria would have overcome me. Strangely, my response was quite muted. I do believe the mind filters and retards the flow of both excessive joy and trauma on the basis that excess of any kind is injurious to the mind.

Summary

1. **Don't ever get ahead of yourself**. Ever since my 'troubles' began I'd been searching in vain for a 'seer' – a wise person who'd give me direction on to how best to respond to this situation. And then I found her. She'd been there all along. Well, almost. My daughter Sarah. The lads had

slagged her that she'd been AWOL during the eye of the storm – the operation. But now that school days in Dubai were over for the summer she was back sitting with me – on a high stool in Linnanes. As we caught up on stuff I began to faff about the histology results and what they might be and she stopped me.

'Dad. You're getting way ahead of yourself. Don't allow yourself do that.'

Had my consultant told me that; or the Bishop of Galway; or even Brian O'Driscoll himself for that matter, I'd have told them where to get off. But there's a sacred connection that exists only between a father and daughter. This was no scientific or theological treatise. This was an innate wisdom that only a daughter could access from the universal intelligence for her Dad in times of trouble.

I understood in that moment, for the first time, what the 'Power of Now' really meant. It transcended intellectual understanding. As the kids say 'I just got it.' It underpinned what Deepak Chopra meant when he said. 'The past is history. The future is a mystery. The present is now which is why it's called a 'present.'

No pint tasted sweeter. No daughter looked more beautiful. No ambience felt more peaceful.

2. **Results are rarely as life defining or cataclysmic as they first appear**. Avoid getting overly hung up on results and outcomes. Failing the Leaving; or getting stood up by the 'special one;' or having your banker tell you he doesn't

agree with your business plan are not necessarily the end of the world.

I love farmers because of their wisdom acquired from observing natural laws. In particular I love Taoist farmers because of their ambivalence to results and outcomes. Here's an old Taoist farmers parable.

This farmer had only one horse, and one day the horse ran away. The neighbours came to him bemoaning his terrible loss. The farmer said, 'Maybe it is. Maybe it isn't!'

A month later, the horse returned home – this time bringing with her two beautiful wild horses. The neighbours rejoiced at the farmer's good fortune! The farmer said, 'Maybe it is. Maybe it isn't!'

The farmer's son was thrown from one of the wild horses and broke his leg. The neighbours were deeply distressed. Such bad luck! The farmer said, 'Maybe it is. Maybe it isn't!'

A war came, and every able-bodied man was conscripted and sent into battle. Only the farmer's son, because he had a broken leg, remained. The neighbours congratulated the farmer on his outstanding luck. 'Maybe it is. Maybe it isn't!' said the farmer.

That farmer knew his onions!

3. **Model people of deep courage and character.** Jim Mitchell had outstanding courage. So equally had the late

Brian Lenihan. They got on with the job in the midst of great personal trauma and put affairs of the nation and the people they served above their own. Lenihan continued to almost singlehandedly keep the Irish economy afloat as his cabinet colleagues dithered lamentably. Lenihan's only concession to his illness and treatment was a couch in his office where he occasionally took naps after his treatment.

Bill Clinton is also worthy of model status. Like him, or like him not, he held his nerve and grace – and ultimately his reputation – in the way he managed the furore following the Monica Lewinsky affair. White House Officials conceded how staggered they were to see him consistently arrive at his desk daily and continue to make sound decisions on behalf of America and the world despite the intense media spotlight on him. Bozo would have loved him.

4. **It's OK to surrender. In fact, sometimes it's wise to surrender.** Last January the Flaggy Shore got pounded and battered by unprecedented bad storms. Buildings and walls constructed from the toughest of limestone, and that had survived for years, were pummelled and flattened. And yet, the reeds that adorn the isolated and bare limestone flags that were in the very eye of the storm, were left largely unharmed. To understand how they survived is to understand how to cope with trouble and life. They refused to resist the destructive storms. They willingly bent and yielded to the force of the wind and as a result were left unscathed when the storm abated.

Sometimes, we too, having done all we can about the scenario in hand, have to let go and let results look after themselves.

5. **Develop a buffalo mindset and ditch the bull mindset.** Nature endows the buffalo naturally with its distinctive coping DNA. It's strategy of minimising its exposure to the storms of life by charging directly into them is clearly sensible. Unfortunately the same is not true of humans. In fact, there's a concerted campaign that promotes the path of least resistance and 'get rich quick' schemes. We have to learn and develop and practice deep rooted habits of Smácht in all our dealings in order to minimise our exposure to problems and pain. The reality is that we'll all face our share of inevitable and unavoidable problems. We can moan about them or solve them. The latter is by far the most productive strategy.

6. **Control the controllable's.** There will be circumstances, people and events that you will have no control over. Let them go. Let them off. On the other hand be aware of what your locus of control is and insist on spending the bulk of your time there.

Chapter 8
Live in the Present Moment

I first came across the concept in Freeney's pub from my late father-in-law, Pat Carroll. A former army general, he'd been one of the first commanders to safely bring troops in and out of the Congo in the 1960s.

On a clean beer mat he explained to me in large letters his mantra for success, not just on military matters, but on all issues pertaining to life and indeed business. Like all great formulae it contained just three components summarised in three letters.

P.D.R. – The letters stood for **Plan. Do. Review.**

He proceeded to join each letter with an arrow thereby signifying a recurring process.

Pat explained that if you applied this formula to all aspects of life from rearing a family, to going on a holiday to building a business that you'd greatly enhance your probability of success.

I introduced the concept in Smácht and it took off swimmingly. Smáchters enthusiastically began to PDR their budgets, daily plans, meetings, performance appraisals, presentations, projections and proposals. The really astute ones began to PDR their health, their relationships and their financial freedom – those aspects of most importance and impact.

It's now a core component of the evolving Smácht body of knowledge. A good place to begin is to review your plan for the last period of your life be that a year, a month, a day or even a minute!

My plans for the past six months were written on a letter I wrote to myself on May 25th of this year – just two days before I heard I had a mass in my heart. They were:

1. Spend two months living and working in Colhoure in the South of France. (We had the idyllic house over-looking the bay and ancient town booked for over six months.)
2. Write a book on one of the world's most exciting young entrepreneurs. (I had this arranged in April and we were both hot to trot for June.)
3. Expand Smácht globally into the UK, Scandinavia and Dubai. (I had the right people on the bus to expedite this.)
4. Kite surf every Saturday morning in Lahinch. (I had developed a great relationship with the best kite surf-ing teacher in Ireland.)

Planning, or decision making, is the first component of success but it is by no means a guarantee of success. My Uncle Stíofáin delighted in the riddle of the three birds.

'Pádraiceen, if there were three birds on a telephone wire and two decided to fly away, how many would there be left?'

'Easy peasy.' I replied without thinking and with complete and utter certainty.

'There'd be one left.'

'Pádraiceen, always remember that there's a world of difference between deciding to do something and actually doing something. Half the woes of the world are caused by people deciding to do things but not following through and actually doing them.'

Like all great storytellers he didn't tell me the answer. He let me figure it out for myself that there were still three birds left on the wire. For years after, as I'd be travelling the country, I'd holler at any random bird I saw on a telephone wire and scream.

'JFDI. (Just F****** Do It.) And believe it or not, most did!

Let me tell you what I did in relation to my goals in the last six months. This, by the way, is the 'Review' component of the PDR formula.

With the exception of getting kite surfing twice before the operation, I did:

Nothing. Nada. Faic. Tada. Zero.

I have however had:

1 Angiogram.
6 Cardiac Ultra Sounds.
1 Head Scan.
7 Chest X Rays.
3 Cardiac MRIs.
2 T.O.E.s (Trans-Oesophageal Echocardiograms)
2 Abdomen Scans.
1 Open Heart Surgery.
1 Cystoscopy.
3 Spinal MRIs.
2 Bone Scans
1 Kidney Ultra Sound.
1 Carotid Scan.

I've consulted with 12 different consultants, have had dozens of blood tests done, and spent 69 nights in hospital on industrial strength antibiotics.

Quite impressive for a guy who'd never been in a hospital before May except as a visitor.

The outcome was that I developed an infection that neither the consultants nor any of the above tests have succeeded in sourcing or identifying. I was treated for a condition called endocarditis which is an infection of the heart wall lining yet which never manifested in any of the blood cultures.

If I'd heard it once, I heard it a dozen times. 'Pádraic, what happened to you is as rare as hens' teeth.'

Seven weeks after the operation I developed a urinary tract infection. Although it's quite common in women it's relatively rare in men. Paddy O'Malley, who pioneered robotic prostate surgery in Ireland, and a good friend of mine, insisted on dragging me back immediately to the Galway Clinic and performing an abdominal scan.

It was hugely disappointing and scary. I'd just survived open heart surgery and gotten out on the right side of a rare growth and now I was having my kidneys scanned. As Anne and I sat in the canteen of the Galway Clinic awaiting Paddy's prognosis I descended into one of the lowest points of my journey. I'd been ready for the operation. I'd been prepared even for bad news on the histology. I was sure I was out the gap. But this. I was totally unprepared for it.

I saw Paddy shuffling up the stairs of the clinic with what I suspected were the results of my scan. There was no small talk.

'Your scan is normal. But do you know what Pádraic, you're condition is as rare as ....'

'Paddy.' I roared, more in pent up jubilation than anything else.

'If someone else tells me my condition is as rare as hens' teeth I'll clock them.'

'No, it's much rarer than that.' He replied flatly.

I hadn't been expecting this. I glanced at Annie timorously and could see her devastation. I faced back to Paddy and thought 'Buffalo.'

'What's it rarer than Paddy?' I asked evenly.

'It's rarer than rocking horse shit.' He replied with a grin as wide as Galway Bay.

It took us a moment to assimilate the meaning and then the implication and then the humour. I loved it and it struck me not for the first time, just how important humour is in the travails of life, and how important it is to get around people with a sense of humour. More specifically, professionals of every hue should be inducted in the basics of humour and encouraged to apply it liberally.

Norman Cousins had extended his terminal cancer prognosis by twenty five years through actively engaging in a regime of constant laughter and merriment. His account in 'Anatomy of an Illness' is compelling evidence of the power of laughter and fun and humour in the healing process. Sadly, modern society, with its preoccupation on targets and objectives and performance measures has succeeded in pushing much of the humour out of living and working. I was appalled recently to learn from a former lecturer of mine, one whose content I can still recall after thirty years, that he'd been hauled over the coals recently for indulging in too much humour and storytelling in his lectures. 'Stick to the content and avoid the anecdotes,' he was advised by a younger student, a third of his age.

I'd planned on returning to work the first week in September but each time that I would plan on returning to work I'd be beset by a fresh resurgence of the infection that would leave me in severe pain, feverish and weak as a kitten. The bottom line was that I had neither the energy nor the focus nor the well-being to do any of my planned goals.

Therefore the big question is whether the PDR formula is futile given the vagaries of life and circumstances.

After much reflection I'm more convinced than ever of the effectiveness of the formula. The only modification I'd make to it is, stop making five year plans, or one year plans, or even one day plans.

MAKE 'ONE MOMENT PLANS.'

Resolve to live in the present moment.

This struck me like a bang on the head one other miserable day in mid-October. My entire life had become a process of waiting. Waiting for the breakfast to arrive. Waiting for the phlebotomist to take bloods. Waiting for the nurses to do their observations. And worst of all, waiting for the consultant to deliver his daily prognostications.

I'd begun to get good at deciphering his news. If he walked in speedily and noisily refusing to engage in banter and conversation the news was bad. If he appeared silently, with a playful smile the news was good or at least neutral.

This particular morning I could tell the news was not of the cheerful variety. My CRP (infection and inflammation levels) were elevated. My renal function had disimproved. And there was an issue about a shadow on my bone marrow. Three different consultants would be visiting me in the next few days. More waiting. More worrying. More woe.

I challenged him by asking him to be more positive with me and immediately regretted it. He had been caring and compassionate and competent in the extreme with me.

'I deal in facts Padraic.'

It was a fair comment and I respected him massively for doing that.

The man in the cubicle beside me had been listening attentively to the prognosis and upon his departure was lavish in his assessment.

'They're not too good are they?' He said unhelpfully.

'What are not too good?' I responded acerbically.

'The facts.' He replied with all the subtlety of a brick.

I was precluded from clocking him mainly due to being tethered by the lines from the intravenous drip pumping vancomycin into my collapsing veins.

He'd set my mind thinking however on the impact of facts on our lives. And bless his innate predilection for doom and gloom but he reminded me of that priceless gem of wisdom from Charles Swindoll.

Attitude is more important than facts. It is more important than the past, than education, money, circumstances, than failures and success, than what other people think, say, or do. It is more important than appearance, ability, or skill. It will make or break a business, a home, a friendship, an organisation. The remarkable thing is I have a choice every day of what my attitude will be. I cannot change my past. I cannot change the actions of others. I cannot change the inevitable. The only thing I can change is attitude. Life is ten percent what happens to me and ninety percent how I react to it.

In that moment I resolved emphatically to forge an attitude of living in the now – in the present moment.

And as my mind transmitted that thought, it was instantly responded to by the words of Robert Anthony.

Ultimately then, there is only one problem in life – not living in the now. If you are constantly focusing on the past or future, you are not using your mind; your mind is using you. If you find it difficult to live in the NOW, try this: Stand back and just observe the habitual tendency of your mind wanting to escape the now. You will observe that the future is usually better or worse than the present. If the imagined future is better, it gives you hope, pleasure and anticipation. If it is worse, it creates anxiety. Both are illusions.

Don't judge or analyse what you observe. Watch the thought – feel the emotion, observe the reaction – become the silent watcher. This will help you to focus on the moment, because the moment you realise you are not present, you ARE present.

What wisdom lies in those few lines!

They inspired me to immediate action. The moment my drip was finished I beseeched the nurse to allow me out to visit 'my poor ailing mother who's heart was broken because of my illness.' She consented on the grounds that I'd stay indoors and not get cold.

I had a plan, and no sooner was I in the car then I phoned my two sons who were home for the week, and ordered them to get the fishing gear ready 'toute suite,' as they say in France. I drove like the clappers to Black Head and within the hour we were casting spinners into the deep waters of Galway Bay.

I lived each one of those moments vividly in the present and there's no telling what we might have caught had my mobile phone not gone off. It was my nurse in the Galway Clinic.

'Pádraic, come in at once. Your creatinine levels are through the roof at 1.6 and the consultants have decided to change the antibiotic.'

A beautiful county, just like a beautiful painting, is best viewed at from a distance. You have to go to the Burren in

County Clare to really appreciate the stunning and diverse beauty of County Galway. Looking westward from Blackhead I could see the three Aran Islands glisten like diamonds in the turquoise coloured waters of the benign Atlantic. To the north west the Twelve Pins stood in purple majesty against the golden glow of the kind Autumn sun. Directly in front of me were the towns of Spiddal and Barna and the coastline of Cois Fhairraige. And to the east was the city of Galway, and further east again was the Galway Clinic, my current residence.

'Pádraic, where in the name of God are you? It sounds as if you're out in a gale!'

'Gods own country.' I replied absentmindedly.

'Where's that you are. I hope you're not out in the cold.'

'Not at all nurse.' I placated her. 'I'm in the hairdressers with the mother. She's having the colour done in the hair and they're drying it at the moment. The only thing is I'll be at least another hour or two.'

Even the man in the cubicle beside me was surprised at my rosy complexion that evening.

The following day I improved on my plan. I told the nurse I had to take the mother to the chiropodist and shaved a good half hour off my journey by fishing in New Quay. It would have worked too had there not been a rising tide and quite the best shoal of mackerel ever seen at that late time of the year. There were only three of us on the Quay

– myself, my son Harry and Pat Molloy. Nothing in the wide world brings you so close to the present moment as hooking and playing a fresh fish. The whole moment pulses and throbs with sensation. Such was the activity and excitement and my preoccupation with the present moment that I lost all sense of time and became oblivious to everything.

It was well past seven when eventually the light failed us and we were compelled to complete our sporting. As we packed away the equipment into the car I noticed a number of missed calls from the Galway Clinic. I listened to the most recent one. 'Pádraic, I need you to call me. A phrenologist, a haematologist and an infectious disease consultant have all been trying to see you and you were AWOL. We need to talk.' It was my consultant.

I concede that for the first time in those few days I failed to live in the present. I became quagmired in the future. What would happen? How would I explain things? Would they evict me from the Clinic? What would the consultants say? Or worse again, my mother, whom I hadn't seen in a month!

Pat Molloy rescued me from the future by hauling me firmly back to the present. He insisted Harry and I join him for a pint whereby he would reveal a foolproof plan to share with my consultant. Pat is the living embodiment of Ernest Hemingway in physique, angling and storytelling prowess.

It was my first pint in weeks and it brought me back very nicely and squarely to the present. Maybe it was that special combination of antibiotics and porter but the future became kind of opaque and distant and eventually I let go of it completely. After the second pint, Pat's plan became crystal clear.

My bedroom was situated immediately behind the nurses station in the cardiac unit of the Clinic. This is ideal for patients who are in need of emergency attention and resuscitation, but a distinct disadvantage to those smelling of fresh fish and porter, attempting to circumnavigate the circular station unnoticed. What's worse, my consultant was there.

I recalled Pat's advice. Seize the initiative.

'We need to talk. Preferably in private,' I intimated, leading him into a vacant consulting room.

'How many patients have you attending your clinic tomorrow morning? I asked assertively.

'I haven't seen the list yet but probably about twelve. Why do you ask?'

'Omega 3 and 6 are extremely powerful in the maintenance of a healthy heart and one of the richest sources of omega oil is fresh mackerel,' I'd begun to say before he interrupted me.

'Pádraic, I'm a consultant physician. Don't you think I know this!'

'Sure I do, but do you know where to get fresh local mackerel in mid-October in Ireland?' I repeated Pat's words verbatim and continued persuasively.

'I want to make a donation of 60 mackerel, freshly caught this afternoon in pristine clear waters, to your patients for tomorrow morning. Imagine the example it will set. They'll develop great eating habits for the rest of their lives.'

Although his instructions to me to remain in the clinic 'til at least 12 noon the next day were non-negotiable, there was no concealing the playful smile. Although I'd lived vicariously in the present and risked censure, I'd managed to get away with it.

That night I slept like a baby.

I was awakened the following morning by a phone call from Pádraig Ó Céidigh, the founder of Aer Arann and the winner of the 2002 Ernst Young Entrepreneur of the Year.

'Pádraic, Cáitlín is after coming down with a bug and can't make the 2014 EY Function in Dublin this evening. Will you be my guest at the function this evening?'

It felt like being asked to a Debs by a lovely person when you were going out with someone equally nice. It was wonderful to be asked but there was something morally wrong about accepting. Ever since the start of my health ordeal, Pádraig had really looked out for me and had called and visited me many times. In addition, the EY Award is quite the biggest and most prestigious business award in Ireland. But I was in hospital. My vital signs were all over the shop. And most worryingly of all, my energy levels were on the floor. What if I couldn't last the pace or let Pádraig down in rarified company? What if the pain became so severe that I had to be hospitalised in Dublin? What if the Clinic found out? And they'd be sure to find out as I wouldn't be back 'til all hours.

And then I realised that anytime you're asking the 'What if' question you're wandering dangerously into 'Future' territory.

'Let the future look after itself,' I heard a cheerful voice exclaim in my head.

'How does it feel now,' the same voice asked.

It felt awesome. And I decided there and then to say yes to the moment and to the universe and to deal with the consequences when, or if, they emerged.

'Pádraig, I'd love to go.'

'Excellent. I'll pick you up at the Clinic at 1 pm. Be sure and have your Tuxedo on as I've a live interview with Newstalk at 5 in Citywest.'

I rang Annie, explained that I was going to a Black Tie function in Dublin that afternoon, and could she bring me in my dress suit with my clean pyjamas.

'You'll never get away with it,' said my Polyanna in the cubicle beside me.

'You what?' I said furiously.

'I couldn't help overhearing you on the phone and you skiving off to a do in Dublin tonight. They went spare here yesterday after you going off with your mother for the day.'

I didn't have time to worry. I willingly allowed myself be prodded and poked by three different consultants.

I asked my favourite nurse if it would be ok if I went to a business meeting with a very important person and assured her I'd stay well away from the cold. As she wrote 'out at business meeting' in my file I somehow neglected to tell her it was in Dublin.

I barely had enough time to slip into my Tux and conceal it beneath my overcoat before it was time to go. I asked Polyanna how I looked and his sneer said it all.

If the previous twelve weeks had been dull, tedious and mundane, the next twelve hours were invigorating, uplifting and game changing. Pádraig looked after me like a baby. I almost ended up on the live Newstalk interview between Bobby Kerr and Pádraig before I remembered just in time that I was supposed to be in hospital.

I spent the drinks reception in the company of sporting legends – Liam Griffin, Joe Connolly and Dessie Farrell. There was champagne flowing like a Spring tide and I was too polite to decline.

As the Awards are recorded at 6 pm and later televised on RTE 1, there was a big kerfuffle to get people seated by 5-45 pm . Pádraig ushered me to our table – the top table – which seated the good and great of corporate Ireland. I needn't have worried about my elevator pitch. Having introduced me to Denis O'Brien, Pádraig blurts out.

'Show him your arm.'

I must say that the ID wristband from the Galway Clinic and the large cannula attached to my arm with six inches of tubing hanging out of it was quite a party piece. The only problem I had all night was remembering to bow my head when the TV camera panned to the top table. While I would dearly loved to have winked at Polyanna, I didn't think it was worth alarming the nursing staff – yet.

The plan was that we were to depart at 9.30 pm and be back in Galway before midnight. The challenge was that Pádraig is Chairman of the Adjudicators and quite the most affable and sociable guy you'd ever meet. I had to show my cannula to a good half of the 1500 gathering before departing Citywest.

It was near enough to midnight when I rang the cardiac ward of the Galway Clinic.

'Where the Hell are you and are you all right?'

I'd rehearsed my lines well.

'My heartbeat is stable. Temperature appears to be normal. And the cannula is holding sound. The only problem is I'm in Dublin and won't get back 'til 2.30 pm.'

In the negotiation component of our Smácht Selling course, we always counsel giving the bad news and then saying nothing. 'Never justify your price,' has saved our clients a fortune over the years.

It worked a great here now. There was a discernible sigh of relief followed by a fresh burst of orders.

'Do not attempt to climb in a window when you get back. You'll set the alarm off and wake the whole hospital. Ring the front door and I'll have security alerted to let you in.'

She was as good as her word and by 2.30 am even Poly anna was impressed with my adventure. Like me, it seemed to have given him renewed life and spirit and hope.

The key question to ask today therefore is:

How am I going to live more in the present moment?

A great technique to enable you do that is to ask 'The W.I.N.' Question.

W.I.N. Is an acronym for 'What's Important Now?'

Each time you ask yourself that question you ground yourself more in the present moment.

Each moment will require a different response. Sometimes the most important thing to do will be to put your head down and slog hard at the task in hand. Other times it will be to take time to sit, do nothing, smell the roses and not feel one iota of guilt about doing so.

Thích Nhất Hạnh, the Vietnamese Zen Buddhist monk, put it far more elegantly and eloquently when he said

> *Drink your tea slowly and reverently, as if it is the axis on which the world earth revolves – slowly, evenly, without rushing toward the future.*

And as for 'Facts.' The following morning I discovered an unopened packet of paracetamol in the inside pocket of my dress suit. In my excitement I had forgotten to take them. Miraculously I had no pain to remind me to take them. And as for my CRPs that morning. They had dropped 25% since the day before.

What was it that the wise man said about attitude being more important than facts?

Chapter 9
Take Responsibility

The right thing to do and the hard thing to do are usually the same.

Steve Maraboli

Long before self service became de rigueur in petrol stations, I subvented my drinking money as a student by filling petrol in Dooley's Esso station opposite the university. It was the quintessential student job – good money, great craic and bugger all responsibility. Or so I thought.

My comrade in arms was a class mate called Paddy Ridge. One evening, the biggest Mercedes we'd ever seen pulled into the forecourt and Paddy proceeded to fill it up. As he filled, the driver chatted amiably about business, student life and career plans.

All would have gone swimmingly had Amy Lally not chosen to strut through the forecourt en route to a Dramasoc rehearsal at precisely that time. Any time Amy strutted her stuff on University Road, the traffic would invariably stutter and inevitably stop. It was said that Amy was the inspiration behind the iconic lines in the Saw Doctors song 'I useta love her'

I useta see her up the chapel when she went to Sunday Mass

And when she'd go to receive, I'd kneel down there
And watch her pass
The glory of her ass

In any event, Paddy was momentarily distracted and inadvertently spilled a dollop of diesel over the drivers immaculate pinstripe suit and hand-stitched Loake loafers. The scowl on the drivers face had a lot in common with the smell and stain of diesel – it was toxic and pungent and unlikely to disappear easily.

I'm always fascinated by the way in which we react or respond in a crisis. It occurred to me in that instant that Paddy had one of three choices: 1. Mutter an excuse about the dodgy fuel line. It actually was leaking. 2. Blame the driver for standing too close to him. 3. Say nothing and hope nothing happened.

Paddy did none of the above.

Looking the driver calmly in the eye he said 'I'm really sorry for spilling that diesel on your clothes. It was completely my fault and shouldn't have happened. Unfortunately it will smell and you do need to get it dry cleaned immediately.'

Taking his wallet out of his pocket, he withdrew the only money he had to his name, a carefully folded fiver and said to the Mercedes owner. 'There's a great dry cleaners in Briar Hill called Bee Green Dry Cleaners. They use completely natural cleaning materials and your suit will be as good as new afterwards. The owner is a man called

Stevie Langan. He's my uncle. Tell him that Paddy Ridge sent you and to look after you. If it's not completely as good as new come back to me and I'll sort it out.'

That was the thing about Paddy. He took 100% responsibility for the results in his life. His immediate response to every circumstance in his life was:

I AM RESPONSIBLE.

When you live and die by the I AM RESPONSIBLE credo there's no room for excuses or blaming or complaining.

These three simple words, if repeated regularly and lived with gusto, will greatly enhance your peace and productivity and prosperity. That is, if you have the courage!

Emblazon those words in your mind now. Roar them out loud. Roll them around your mouth as you would a fine wine perfectly chambréd.

For these words are the panacea to all and every form of procrastination and prevarication.

Imagine if you were to take 100% responsibility for every result in your life right now – positive and negative! That would entail never blaming circumstances, luck or people for any of the outcomes in your life. Try it for the next 24 hours.

I AM RESPONSIBLE.

When you front up to life and take full responsibility for it, you eliminate much of the scope for excuses, blaming and victimisation.

Whilst many of our B. Comm class aspired to getting a good job, Paddy ended up owning an entire chain of garages in the UK. Whilst half of UCG (the entire male half) dreamed of courting Amy Lally, Paddy Ridge ended up marrying her. And whilst many of us are still ducking and diving and making excuses, Paddy is a free man because he always believed and practiced the credo:

I AM RESPONSIBLE.

Responsibility, like routines, comes before results.

But do you know what?

Life is tough.

And paradoxically, the sooner you suck that up, the easier life becomes.

The late John O'Donohue discovered this as a young lad planting a fence post in the limestone topography of his beloved Burren. He'd been helping his father repair a damaged fence after a violent storm and he was finding it nigh impossible to locate an easy place to sink the fence post. It seemed every place he attempted to impale the post was hard and difficult to pierce. Just then he discovered a mound of soft grass and sand where the post descended almost effortlessly. To his dismay his father promptly told him to take it out explaining that 'That post went down far too easily John. There was no resistance. In the next big wind it will be the first to topple over.'

And so it is with us. We spend vast swathes of our lives seeking out the quick fix, the easy way out, the short cut. We then become disillusioned when it rains on our parade and so many of our dreams and goals end up being toppled by the storms of life.

I had a sudden seizure of 'POM' (Poor Old Me) Syndrome myself at the start of the year. Being January 5th 2015, it was the first Monday of the New Year and the first day back to work for many. The presenter on the radio was reading out a series of POM texts concerning people's gloom regarding returning to work after the Christmas holidays.

For thirty odd years I'd been culpable of much the same moaning and groaning. This year I would have given a king's ransom to have been heading back to work. Instead, I began the year in a consultants waiting room in the Galway Clinic.

The consultant as always was caring and compassionate and competent. But it failed utterly to sweeten the taste of returning to hospital for another ten blood tests and facing another period of uncertainty and insecurity.

The consultation left me with little stomach for coffee and scones and even less so for letting blood in phlebotomy. Instead I ambled aimlessly into the Oratory of the Clinic as I'd done countless times in my protracted stay there. Over time I'd come to cherish this haven of tranquillity located in a desert of sickness and disease. I allowed the amber and golden light from the exquisite stained glass windows wash over my spirit. Unlike the vast and cold and austere Monastery in Roscrea, this sanctuary was small and modern and intimate. I could imagine a fashion writer describing it as 'bijou.' I felt if God was here at all, I had him well cornered, and he couldn't escape me without a good struggle and I fully intended venting on him about 'POM.'

I began with the left ventricular non-compaction issue, followed by; the calcified atrial tumour; the open heart surgery; the urinary tract infection; the current infection that the best medics in the country can't source. I then gave him the twin barrels with my financial woes precipitated by not having worked for six months. I abused him rightly about probably having to reschedule Smácht Mór until after the upcoming tests were completed and the further damage this could do to my reputation.

I succeeded in working myself up in to a storm of panic and fear.

And as you'd expect, nada happened. I'd hoped for a miracle, a spontaneous remission, an apparition from a friendly saint. I'd have even settled for an intuitive understanding.

But at least it had felt good to dump.

And I'd have probably begun in earnest again had the door not opened and a very attractive nurse escorting a very shook looking man entered in a wheelchair.

I averted my eyes. And although I recognised the man immediately I was appalled to see how he'd deteriorated since last I'd seen him. We'd shared a room together in the Clinic before Christmas and I learned a little about his story.

Just over a year ago, he'd returned from America with his wife where they'd both worked for the past forty years. The dream of an idyllic retirement dissipated fast. They found it difficult to settle in Ireland and many of their original friends and family had left or died. His own wife died within six months leaving him without his soul mate. And in November last he himself had suffered a stroke that had seriously disabled him and would likely finish him.

Despite his travails he never let it get him down or effect his attitude.

I watched him focus and connect with the altar and noticed his physiology changing. His body straightened; his eyes softened; and at times, a trace of a smile bookended his lips.

And as the nurse was wheeling him out he caught my eye and flashed me a beaming smile. 'Like my new girl friend?' he quipped.

As Chris DeBurg so memorably sang in the ditty 'Spanish Train,' 'Just then The Lord himself appeared, in a blinding flash of light.'

Like Paddy Ridge, this sick patient had taken 100% responsibility for his life, his circumstances and his attitude. He refused resolutely to bitch or moan or whinge. He persisted in behaving with dignity and purpose and humour even amidst the most harrowing of circumstances. People like these refuse to do POM or feel sorry for themselves. They live and die with the mantra.

I AM RESPONSIBLE.

The smile and dignity and presence of that dying man had banished any lingering wimpish self-pity and awoken within me an infinity of possibilities and opportunities. I had a new lease of life.

I uttered the words silently to myself a number of times and immediately felt them kick in providing courage and vigour and wisdom.

I AM RESPONSIBLE.

I whispered to myself.

I AM RESPONSIBLE.
I AM RESPONSIBLE FOR GETTING WELL AGAIN
AND REINVENTING MY CAREER.

There came the inevitable charge of the Doom Brigade – my wild ponies.

'Given that the cause of your infection has so far baffled and confounded the best medics in the country, how are you possibly going to get well again? And as for reinventing your career, you haven't the energy to make a phone call some days not to mind giving a talk for four hours. You're SHAGGED.'

The connectivity to the Divine WiFi improved out of all recognition.

From every recess of that sacred ground reverberated the words of Mark in 11:24.

'Therefore I say unto you, What things soever ye desire, when ye pray, believe that ye receive them, and ye shall have them.'

Although I hadn't realised I was even praying my prayers had miraculously been answered. Business consultants are obsessed with processes and formulae and I now had a process and a formula for manifestation.

I explained it in lay man's terms to my wild horses.

'What things soever ye desire,' literally means to be clear about what you want, as opposed to being clear about what you don't want. Up to now I've been ambivalent and negative about getting well again and reinventing my career.

'When ye pray,' means to ask with intention and purpose. For the last six months I've been waiting and hoping as opposed to asking and demanding and insisting.

And this is the piece de resistance. 'Believe that ye receive.' This means believing without seeing or having evidence. In olden days it would have called 'faith' but it's the panacea for all manifestation.

I summarised by telling them that in life you can either be a victim or a wizard. Victims bitch and moan and whinge. They refuse to take responsibility. Wizards, on the other hand, create magic. They take responsibility. From this moment forward

I AM RESPONSIBLE FOR GETTING WELL AGAIN
AND REINVENTING MY CAREER.

They didn't like it one little bit. I said I'd elaborate on it in the next chapter.

As I departed the Oratory I glanced up at the words of St Paul inscribed above the door.

Sickness brings patience,
Patience brings perseverance,
Perseverance brings hope.

I Am Responsible

I am responsible.
For every result in my life.
For every failure and every victory.
For every time I flounder, function and flourish.
I am responsible for my state of mind.
For the choices I make consciously, and those I do not make.
I accept implicitly that I am precisely as happy and fulfilled
And as successful as I make my mind up to be.
I am responsible for the oomph in my life.
When people love me, I am responsible.
When they resist me, I am responsible.
Always my choice.
I am responsible for the buzz in my life.
Newton was on the money when he said that
For every action there is an opposite and equal reaction.
I pamper my body with daily vigorous exercise and great food.
And it responds exactly.
I am responsible for the money in my life.
When I'm broke I am responsible.
When I'm flush, I take all the credit.
Either way, I know there's more than enough money to
Satiate my every need. All I need to do is be responsible.
I am responsible for where I live right now.
At times I've lived in the past but it's history.
At times I've lived in the future but it's a mystery.
I choose to live in the present. To accept every event and
Person as they are, not as how I'd like them to be.
I am responsible for being either a victim or a wizard.
Victims bitch and blame and make excuses.
Wizards believe in the supreme magic of responsibility.
Magic is the process of producing remarkable results.
I AM RESPONSIBLE.

Chapter 10
Get a Great S.H.A.G.

The text really irked me.

All it said was 'P, what would make 2012 a really significant year for you? You don't ever need to tell me. Just write it down.'

It annoyed me for a number of reasons.

Firstly, I was seriously hung over. We have old Junior Chamber friends over every first Friday of the New Year and this year it had inadvertently spilled over into the Saturday. It had begun innocently enough in Linnanes with the intellect of the party, one John Keyes, recommending 'LTPs for medicinal reasons.' 'LTPs' is JC parlance for 'Lunch Time Pints,' and they were efficacious in the extreme. These were followed gently by 'MAPs' which refer to 'Mid-Afternoon Pints' as opposed to those instruments of navigation. These were proceeded with increased vigour by 'TTPs' which as you've probably surmised, stand for 'Tea Time Pints.' Then we went on the lash.

Secondly, the text arrived early on the following Sunday morning, ostensibly the day of rest. Thirdly, it came from a person I greatly respected.

What vexed me most however, was that I had no answer to that question. And like most great things in life that question requires grounded thought and reflection and going within. And it's infinitely far too powerful a question to leave unanswered.

A suitable answer eluded me hopelessly all that day. With the sobriety of Monday morning, I made time and space and focus to reflect upon and answer that question. And then I wrote myself a letter containing those goals; addressed it to myself; and posted it to myself.

It should have come as no surprise that 2012 was a wonderful year for Annie and I and that most of those goals materialised and manifested. Smácht flourished. The kids did mighty. And we lived and loved and learned a great deal.

Following my epiphany in the Oratory, I repaired with renewed gusto and vigour to the Flaggy Shore for a great S.H.A.G. And before you do likewise, please acquaint yourself firstly with the background and techniques of a S.H.A.G. It will reward your endeavours handsomely.

The first S.H.A.G. was conceived at a Smácht session where I'd been describing the wonderful work of Jim Collins who wrote the iconic book *From Good to Great*. Jim discovered that every great organisation that had ever gone from good to great had what he termed a BHAG – a Big Hairy Audacious Goal. As I was espousing the virtues of having a BHAG, one of our most erudite and accomplished Smáchters of all time, Adrian McKenna, was shaking his head.

'I don't agree Pádraic,' said Adrian apologetically.

'What do you mean Adrian? Collins, an esteemed Professor of Management, has proven categorically that BHAGs work.'

'That may well be the case,' said Adrian, the most affable and civil of people. 'I often had BHAGs and I have to concede, they just didn't work out for a number of reasons.'

Adrian, a partner with Moore Stephens McNamara Accountants in Limerick, did what every decent accountant does. He gave the group example after example of failed BHAGs in his personal and professional life.

I quickly lost the dressing room, and was considering my response when Adrian solved the issue for me.

'Do you know what would work though Pádraic?'

'What Adrian.' I asked hopefully.

'Number 1,' He proceeded, in the vernacular of great accountants. 'Goals are great. The best businesses and individuals all have clearly defined goals. But goals by themselves are little else other than pipe dreams at worst or written on paper at best, and as we all know, paper never refused ink.'

The group clucked in agreement.

'Secondly, what's paramount to making goals work is accountability. When I did achieve one of my BHAGs, cycling from Limerick to Kilkee, I couldn't have achieved it without the accountability of training with my son Ronan. There were countless mornings when it would have been preferable to stay in bed had I not committed to cycling with my son and that was the tipping point in getting me to get up.'

The group were applauding and I didn't know where things were going.

'Thirdly, goals do need to have suction, potency and scale. They need to be 'Hairy.' The reason many of my clients fail is that they have impotent goals. They're not scary enough. If your goals fail to scarify you, they're not real goals.'

Finally, you need to have Smácht (discipline) in abundance to achieve any goal of significance.

The group applauded wildly and I gratefully took notes. I summarised them with a marker on the flip chart.

'Smácht Hairy Accountable Goals.'

The greatest legacy of Smácht has been the quality and quantity of SHAGs that Smácht members have achieved using this simple yet dynamic process. There is irrefutable evidence that goal setting and tracking works.

Like all great processes, it continues to evolve and develop and the following is the latest five phase version of S.H.A.G. Planning.

1. **Get uncomfortable with your current reality**. The two great motivators in life are pain and pleasure. We are genetically programmed to gravitate from one to the other. Consider for a moment a typical frog. If you throw it in to a saucepan of boiling water, it will automatically and immediately jump out. If however, you immerse the frog in a saucepan of cool water and gradually bring it to the boil one degree at a time, the frog will remain there and die.

This is true at a human level also. If we are propelled into an adverse situation, we become very focused and creative in extricating ourselves from it. The danger is when we discover ourselves in situations where things are changing only very slowly and imperceptibly. Situations that were once safe or even pleasurable can have become toxic or odious – one degree at a time. This can happen in business, in careers, in health and in relationships.

The key is to beam a laser of awareness on your current reality. Jim Collins refers to it as 'Confronting the brutal facts.' Two simple but powerful questions to assist you in doing this are:

A. What's working well in my life, business, career, health relationship currently?
B. What's not working well in these areas?

Then associate massive pain with not changing and massive pleasure with changing. This is ultimately the leverage of change.

I had my period of intense pain and discomfort in the Oratory as I indulged in my POM wallowing.

2. Conduct a SWOT Analysis in each of these areas. SWOT is the acronym used in strategic planning denoting 'Strengths, Weaknesses, Opportunities and Threats.' Many people and organisations belittle this process on the basis that it's archaic and that they did it once before. SWOT Analysis is not an ad hoc, once off theoretical exercise. It is a dynamic process that can deliver extremely practical results.

One wonderful practical example of applied SWOT Analysis is to be found in JK Rowling's commencement address to the students of Harvard. Having described her 'current reality' as an almost destitute lone parent who'd severely disappointed her parents, she hit 'rock bottom.

> *I was set free, because my greatest fear had already been realised, and I was still alive, and I still had a daughter whom I adored, and I had an old typewriter and a big idea. And so rock bottom became the solid foundation on which I rebuilt my life.*

Mirroring the process of JK Rowling, I immediately began an audit and inventory of what I had as opposed to what I didn't have.

I had survived three life-threatening episodes in the last six months and was still alive to tell the tale albeit not firing on all cylinders. I had a family who loved me and supported me despite all my idiosyncrasies and foibles and bunions. And I had a story that one cerebral consultant described as being 'as rare as rocking horse shit.'

And that became the basis of my SHAG.

3. Decide exactly what you want or your burning desire. Helen Keller poignantly once said that 'The most pathetic person in the world is someone with sight but no vision.'

I loved that quotation for years before ever realising the full significance of what it really meant.

That would change irrevocably one morning in 1993.

I was part of a NUI Galway Management Development Team providing business training in Russia and my role was to manage the morale of young Irish Marketing Research Graduates.

One of the great attractions of Russian life to young and single male graduates at the time was a flourishing trade in 'blind dating'. It was not at all uncommon for average enough looking Irish lads to meet stunning and receptive Russian beauties – whom it must be said were as partial to western currency and what it could acquire, as to the attractiveness and suitability of the young Irish lads!

Group morale was my responsibility however, and blind dating could justifiably be referred to as a 'morale boosting activity.' I gave it a smidgen of academic credibility by facilitating a review session over coffee each morning with the entire team where events of the preceding evening were discussed and learnings evaluated.

This particular morning two young graduates, Jarlath and Mike, were recalling their first experience of a blind date in Russia.

'It was like this Pádraic. Myself and Jarlath went to the hotel where we were to meet our two dates. Everything went to plan and we met the two girls as arranged'.

'Well what were they like'? roared one over exuberant classmate.

'I'll tell you now without one word of a lie what they were like' said a composed and contrite Mike.

'Jarlath's was a vision. Mine was a sight'.

Now that you too understand the subtle nuances between 'sight' and 'vision' I encourage you to reflect on your goal or vision. The trick here is to state your goal in the present tense as if it's already happened. This is important as your brain is incapable of distinguishing between what's real and imagined.

I frequently get groups to imagine biting into a juicy luscious lemon. It's amazing to witness some extremely intelligent and cynical people testify that their mouths had begun to salivate. This illustrates the power of the imagination. It can induce billions of biochemical changes in your body instantly.

And this works positively and negatively. You can kill yourself or cure yourself by the power of your imagination.

In the greatest treatise written on the process and power of goal setting, Earl Nightingale stated in 'The Strangest Secret', that it's imperative to write your goal down.

For me I wrote that my SHAG statement was.

'I am radiantly healthy and the bestselling writer of the iconic book 'As Rare as Rocking Horse Shit.'

4. **Find a Smácht Cara**. For years I've been intrigued by the Weigh Watchers story. For starters, it's a phenomenal business model. I spend considerable periods of my life in hotels giving talks and it never ceases to amaze me how busy Weigh Watchers are. Secondly, their process works. If you want to lose weight – your goal – they'll increase greatly your chances of doing that.

They do that via a number of interventions but the one that impresses me most is that they weigh you weekly. Think about that. In Irish, it's called 'Freagracht', literally meaning 'Answerability.' The English version is 'Accountability' and it's the fulcrum of achievement. With accountability, we show up, own up and take action. Without it we 'no show,' make excuses and do nothing.

If you're seriously committed to achieving your goal, find a buddy who'll hold you answerable or accountable for the attainment of that goal. In Smácht we call them a 'Smácht Cara' (discipline friend) and they're key to everything you'll ever achieve in life.

Agree on a specific time weekly to review the actions you took that week and to plan actions for the upcoming week. This can be done in person but equally as effectively via phone or Skype.

5. Visualise the successful completion of your goal daily. As part of your daily morning ritual, allow yourself the opportunity of guided visualisation. Induce a relaxed state of mind and picture in multi-sensory detail the attainment of your goal. What will be happening? Who will be there? What are you seeing, hearing or feeling? Intensify the size and clarity and volume of each of these dreams. Bring them closer to you and combine them with music.

In conclusion, there is a very thin line between success and failure. The difference is goals. Brian Tracy said 'Success is goals and everything else is commentary.' Earl Nightingale defined success as 'the progressive realisation of worthy ideals. A success is anyone who is pursuing deliberately a predetermined goal, because that's what he or she decided to do … deliberately.'

I love that expression 'worthy ideals.' A worthy ideal is a school kid doing their homework; a mother raising a family; or an entrepreneur building a business.

When we have 'worthy ideals' we are motivated, energised, fulfilled and on fire.

Nightingale likens the human mind to that of a farmer planting seeds in the land. 'The human mind is far more fertile, far more incredible and mysterious than the land, but it works the same way.

It does not care what we plant ... success ... or failure. A concrete, worthwhile goal ... or confusion, misunderstanding, fear, anxiety, and so on. But what we plant must return to us. The human mind is the last great unexplored continent on Earth.

Chapter 11
The Power of Beliefs

One person with a belief is equal to a force of ninety-nine who have only interests.

John Stuart Mill

It had taken me all of three years to train my Labrador not to retrieve the fowl oven ready.

And today, for the first time, the Smácht had paid off. In a clump of heather, beneath a sheer cliff face in the Burren, he displayed textbook behaviour. His tail arched and pointed to the sky alerting me to the location of his prey. With his eyes, he mesmerised the bird into a state of total immobilisation like a rabbit blinded in the glare of a head-light. All he needed was the command from me, and the bird was as good as in the bag.

Potter could be forgiven for not knowing it was mid-Spring, and that my gun was safely ensconced at home in it's security case obediently awaiting the opening of the shooting season the following September. He was singu-larly unimpressed when I gently ushered him aside and stooped to see what he'd discovered. There, amidst the fronds of heather was a magnificent bird of prey. It peered out at us with beautiful but scarified eyes of amber yellow. One of it's wings hung limply by its side. Clearly, it had fallen from one of the cliffs overhead and had been abandoned by its mother.

Instinctively I thought of Ronan Byrne, the Friendly Farmer. No one in Ireland knows more about birds and their well-being. I resolved to bring the bird to Ronan at once.

'It's an eagle chick and it's in bad shape. The best that we can do with it now is put it in with the other chickens and let nature take its course' said Ronan emphatically.

And that's precisely what happened. We christened the eagle chick Iolar and over the proceeding weeks and months she flourished. She got on like the proverbial house on fire with the other hens and chickens. In time she learned to peck like a chicken, scratch like a chicken, strut like a chicken. She even succeeded in clucking and cackling like a chicken when one of the others laid an egg.

And then one day, a large shadow appeared over the chicken farm in Athenry. Iolar and the other chickens paused momentarily from scratching and looked up to see a majestic bird glide over the farm.

'What's that' said Iolar in awe.

'That's an eagle' said one of the elder and wiser chickens.

'Wow. I'd give anything to fly and soar like that' said Iolar.

'You can't' said another older and wiser chicken.

'You're a chicken, and chickens can't fly. That there is the king of all birds. Now put your head down lest the eagle see you and take you away.'

Iolar dutifully began to scratch the ground again but couldn't take her mind of the spectacular specimen she had just seen.

Some days after, the big eagle happened to be cruising the vicinity of the farm again, and with the aid of his 'eagle eye' he was stunned to see what he perceived to be the prettiest eagle he'd ever seen – hanging out with a bunch of chickens. He surged earthwards with such velocity that the chickens scarcely had time to make the safety of the chicken coop.

Alas, not Iolar. She was so enthralled by the power and splendour of the eagle that she stood transfixed and rooted to the ground.

'What are you doing here?' asked the big eagle curiously but gently.

'What are you getting at?' replied Iolar with false bravado.

'What are you doing hanging out with a bunch of chickens?'

'I am a chicken. They are my friends. They are my family. They took me in when I was abandoned by my mother.

They've taught me everything I know.' said Iolar defiantly.

'You're not a chicken. You're an eagle. You're the king of all birds. From Caesar to Hitler to Hotel California you are revered as the ultimate symbol of power. You belong in the sky, not in the dirt.'

'Nonsense' shrieked Iolar. 'I'm no eagle. I can't even fly.'

'You can't fly because you've never tried, and you've never been coached by someone who can. Come with me to the cliff at the edge of the farm and I'll teach you to fly like an eagle.'

From the recesses of the chicken coop Iolar heard a rising cacophony of chicken speak from the other chickens.

'Don't listen to him' chorused the frenetic chickens. 'He's a lier, a spoofer and a womaniser. If you go with him you'll never come back. If you jump from that cliff you'll surely die. Stay with us here where everything is cosy and safe.'

Iolar looked back at her adopted family and friends and tears welled up in her eyes of amber gold. She thought of all the great times she had scratching in the dirt and scurrying away from Ronan when he tried to tuck them in at night safe from the fox.

But deep within her spirit was a haunting calling. A calling to be more. To do more. To have more. To fly – who knows, even to soar.

She bravely gave the other chickens the wings up and followed the older eagle out of the farmyard and up to the cliff.

At the cliff summit, the boy eagle caringly put his wing around Iolar's graceful shoulders and pointed out all the wonders of an eagle's world. To the north was Croagh Patrick and the Twelve Pins and to the south were the majestic peaks of the Magillicuddy Reeks. Iolar felt an intense stirring in her loins.

Just then the boy eagle jumped – and effortlessly glided on a series of invisible thermals that powerfully supported his body. Iolar marvelled at such unadulterated freedom and dominion over all he purveyed and dearly wished to do likewise.

She looked down however, and all she saw were the sharp and treacherous rocks hundreds of feet below. She heard once again, the clarion cry of the other chickens squawking 'if you jump from that cliff you'll surely die.'

'Look to the sun, throw your heart over the cliff and let me guide you every flap of the way' said the boy eagle encouragingly.

And she did. And as she soared into the heavens her triumphant cry reverberated joyously around the walls of the chicken coop in Athenry.

****

I love that parable for a number of reasons.

It reveals to us that all personal breakthroughs have their genesis in a change of beliefs. Beliefs are to your mind what software is to your computer. They are the programmes that condition and predicate your entire destiny.

And your beliefs are fashioned and fossilised in the 'chicken yards' of your life.

If you ever believed that you're not old enough, smart enough, good looking enough – then it's quite likely you've been got at by 'chicken yard beliefs'.

It's a fascinating fact of life that genetically we are born to win but quickly become programmed to lose – in the 'chicken yards of life.'

The only thing is, as Zig Ziglar reminded us, you'll never soar with the eagles if you continue to scratch with the chickens. It's your choice.

Tony Robbins defines a belief wonderfully by describing it as 'a feeling of certainty about something.' In other words, you believe or feel certain, that you're fit, healthy and intelligent or alternatively that you are overweight, sick or stupid. The inherent power of a belief according to Robbins is that 'Belief delivers a direct command to your nervous system. When you believe something is true, you literally go into the state of it's being true. That sense of certainty allows you to tap into resources that allow you to produce intelligent results. We all have the answers inside us to do virtually anything – or at least we have access to the answers we need through others. But often our lack of belief, our lack of certainty, causes us not to be able to use the capacity that resides within us.'

The key question therefore is how do we change our beliefs?

I believe Iolar, the eagle, provides us with five solutions and I'll add one that is beyond the brain of a bird.

1. **Change the people you're surrounded by**. The quote I have used more than any other in 25 years of business mentoring is that 'You are the average of the five people you are surrounded by most of the time' (Jim Rohn). It is that important that I'll dedicate the next chapter entirely to it.

Suffice to say for now that if you want anything in life it makes implicit sense to get around people who have achieved what you want and you disassociate from those who have failed to achieve what you want.

Iolar would never have ventured near the cliffs were she to have continued to listen to the other chickens limiting beliefs.

Currently I am identifying people who have been cured from diseases similar to mine and drawing on their example and reference to support my new belief system of being well again. In addition, I am reading about and getting around people who have succeeded in setting up online product businesses.

2. **Change your environment.** Why is it that Kerry win the All Ireland Football Final most years and that Kilkenny win the Hurling All Ireland most years and that Blackrock College win the Leinster Schools Senior Cup most years? Is it because they have better players than Mayo or Galway or Cistercian College Roscrea, who struggle so desperately to win?

The main reason is that success breeds success and creates a positive expectation that success will be replicated again. When you're a footballer from Kerry or a hurler from Kilkenny, everyone around you expects you to win and so do you. It becomes a self-fulfilling prophesy.

David McClelland, the former Professor of Management in Harvard, concluded after 25 years' research, that 'your reference group, more than any other factor, determines your destiny.'

At a personal level, in terms of getting well again, I have been making every conceivable attempt to avoid hospitals. With every respect to the wonderful people who work there, disease and sickness and suffering are never too far away. I prefer to go to rugby matches and business conferences and lively pubs to plug in to the vibrancy and positivity. I intend visiting America in February to meet with the top Facebook Marketing people in the world to supercharge my beliefs around my marketing abilities.

Iolar loved her environment. Ronan was a second father to her, her coop was cosy and comfortable and the other chickens treated her royally. That's the thing about environments. They can be so deceptively comfortable that they can blinker us to the possibilities of greater things. Sometimes however, you need to cut the umbilical cord on the past, and step out boldly and confidently into pastures new.

3. **Change the people you model**. It's possibly Tony Robbins' most recurring theme. 'The way to expand our lives is to model the lives of those people who are already succeeding.'

And by modelling them he means getting down and dirty into their belief systems. Elicit what exactly are their beliefs in the area you're trying to change. Interview them. Study them. Live with them.

Iolar would never have flown without understanding the beliefs of the boy eagle.

Right now, in health terms I am modelling my friend Liam Ryan who was given a month to live 13 years ago and who is still running marathons for fun all over the world. In the online product arena, I am modelling Brian Tracy who continues to prodigiously promote excellent content through a series of online programmes.

It was once thought impossible to run a mile in under four minutes because people's belief systems were influenced by the 'flat world' belief that no one had done it before. Within one year after Roger Bannister broke the 'impossible' barrier, 37 other runners did so. The following year, over 300 runners boasted the same.

The only difference was a change of belief in what was possible. Make it your business to model the Roger Bannister of your goal.

4. Do the thing and you'll have the power (of belief). For most of my life I believed I was a terrible runner. And the evidence was there. A friend of mine then described me to my wife as 'your husband's a crap runner.' It created massive motivation for me to change and prove him wrong and I did. I persevered, quite slowly, until I succeeded in running a half marathon. Now I believe I can run, albeit slowly.

Once you successfully accomplish a task or a goal, you have hardwired your brain and belief system to enable you to do it again.

Iolar will never doubt that she can fly again.

5. Fake it 'till you make it. No one espouses the power of affirmation better than Mohammed Ali. In an interview with Michael Parkinson, he once proclaimed 'I said I was 'The Greatest' long before I ever was the greatest.'

Changing beliefs requires focused affirmation, visualisation and mental rehearsal. Ali also said on the same theme. 'It's the repetition of affirmations that leads to belief. And once that belief becomes a deep conviction things begin to happen.'

In sickness, as in business, there is a masse of evidence supporting the power of expectation and positive visualisation in the healing and remission of disease. Carl Simonton, co-author of the bestselling classic *Getting Well Again*, and himself an oncologist, had phenomenal success with terminally ill patients by getting them to adapt empowering beliefs regarding their condition.

He taught patients a simple visualisation technique of firstly relaxing the mind and body and then mentally picturing the cancer, or diseased area, as a series of weak and confused cells. Then he had them picture their body's white blood cells entering the area, recognising the abnormal cells and destroying them. In addition, he had patients believe that the white blood cells were stronger and smarter than the diseased cells and that they would win the battle.

Cynics will tell you, and I can empathise with them, that it's extremely difficult to imagine your disease atrophying when in actual fact it's intensifying. Simonton explained that 'We are attempting to help the patient visualise the desired outcome, not what may be happening at the time. It is possible to picture the cancer shrinking even when in reality it may be growing; you are picturing in your mind what you want to come about.'

Many years earlier, a French pharmacist called Émile Coué, who was curing up to 10,000 people a year, espoused a similar philosophy. He had his patients say the mantra 'Everyday in every way I'm getting better and better' repeatedly.

The discipline of visualisation applies not just to the areas of health and business but also to sport. It is well documented that Bob Bowman, Michael Phelps' coach, had Phelps' mother repeat a guided visualisation picturing the ideal race to the young Phelps each night. Phelps continued to use this technique prior to every race as an adult.

6. **Audit your dominant beliefs**. Tony Robbins makes a distinction between 'Empowering' beliefs and 'Disempowering' beliefs and posits that we should increase our focus on the former and decrease it on the latter. It's an excellent exercise.

On a page, create two columns, and title one 'Limiting Beliefs' and the other 'Empowering Beliefs.' Brainstorm a list of beliefs for each column. Then apply 80:20 analysis to it by identifying the 'vital few and the trivial many' that are most critical to the attainment of your goals. It is a universal law that 20% of the inputs account for 80% of the outputs. The trick is to identify the 'vital few.'

Proceed then to decrease the intensity of the limiting beliefs and correspondingly, increase the intensity of your empowering beliefs. It is possible to conduct this exercise for both you as a person and similarly your team or organisation.

This technique is beyond the capacity of Iolar but one of the most effective personal and corporate training interventions you can take.

In conclusion, beliefs create your behaviour which in turn drives your results and outcomes. One of the reasons that many people fail to deliver on their goals is that their goals and beliefs lack congruency. Your ability to achieve the results you desire in life is commensurate with the intensity of belief you ascribe to them. Henry Ford put it best when he said. 'Whether you think that you can, or that you can't, you are usually right.'

Chapter 12
Get The Right People on Your Bus

All the great minds and scribes are agreed on one elemental component of success. You become like those you associate with.

In Connemara, they'll tell you that 'aithníon cíaróg cíaróg eile.' Scientists will translate this as 'like attracts like' or 'birds of a feather flock together'.

On the street where I live, they have their own way of putting it: 'Lie down with dogs and you'll end up with fleas'.

The trick therefore, is to be consciously aware of the company you keep, and to manage it accordingly. The following vignette underpins how best to become conscious of the Law of Association.

Juliette Murphy was at her hairdressers getting the ubiquitous 'curly blow dry' in advance of a surprise trip to Rome. Unwittingly, she couldn't resist sharing her excitement with the hairdresser.

'You're going to Rome! said the hairdresser pityingly.

'I wouldn't go there if you paid me. One client of mine said it's filthy dirty, outrageously expensive and the Italians'd take the eye out of your head. As a matter of interest, how are you going?

'Ryan Air'

'Ryan Air' said the hairdresser, visibly horrified. 'You'll be packed on top of each other like sardines, you won't get a drop to drink, and the flight will invariably be late. Do you know where you're staying?

'I'm staying in a wonderful boutique hotel across from the Trevi Fountain called 'Bellisimo.'

'Bellisimo' did I hear you say! Another of my clients stayed in the very same place and it was a kip. What are you planning on doing when in Rome?

'I've an audience with the Pope and I'd give anything to shake his hand'.

'Yea sure. You and another million like you. From what I hear from my clients who know, you'll be so far away from him you'll need binoculars to see him'.

About a month after, Juliette returned to the salon for a 'straight do' that apparently was all the rage in Rome.

'How was Rome? enquired the hairdresser knowingly. 'I suppose it was awful'.

'It was wonderful' said Juliette. 'The flight was over-booked and I was upgraded to First Class where I met a dashing Italian pilot who looked after me for the week. The hotel was also over booked and we were upgraded to the Presidential suite. What a blast!

'I bet you didn't get next or near the Pope though' said a clearly unimpressed hairdresser.

'That was the best of all' gushed Juliette. 'As I was waiting in St. Peter's prior to our audience with the Pontiff, a dapper Swiss Guard singled me out and explained that the Pope liked to meet with a sample of visitors to personally deliver a message. I couldn't believe it when I was escorted to a private annex and told that the Pope would be with me in a few minutes.'

'And sure enough, three minutes later, the Pope himself appeared through the door and embraced me warmly and caringly. As I knelt down in reverence and awe, he whispered into my ear nine simple words that I'll never forget.

'What did he say,? said the hairdresser with mounting interest.

He said: 'Who, in the name of God, did your hair?'

****

The above tale illustrates that misery loves company.

So also does joy and abundance and uplifting company. What you end up experiencing in business and life is predicated by the company you keep.

The trick is, just like Juliette, to become conscious of who you associate with and how you do it.

Jim Rohn suggests three levels of association: dis-association; limited association; expanded association.

Dis-association

There are some people who are evil, destructive and psychopathic. There are others who are simply emotional vampires. They suck every scintilla of energy from you. Dis-associate with both species. At once. Now. And forever.

I recall one afternoon going to the canteen of the Galway Clinic with Annie and our son Oige when my fever was sky high. Oige and I sat at a table while Annie was getting the coffee. Had I not been drugged to the gills I'd have seen her coming and eluded her at pace.

She was a friend of the family and she proceeded to sit at our table.

'You're not in the Clinic, a fine strong lad like you! She proclaimed with alacrity.

I had pyjamas on; a dressing gown; slippers; a mobile drip; and a cannula hanging out of my arm. I had everything bar a sign to say

'I am a patient.'

I switched the subject acerbically.

'What's the weather like out there today.'

The sarcasm was totally lost on her and rolled off her like water off a duck's ass. She began to swoon in ecstasy as she commenced to regale us about her husband who was visiting some poor consultant in the Clinic.

Before Annie had returned with the coffee, I had gotten up and returned to bed. The lady appeared neither to be overly aware of my sudden departure or offended at my appalling manners and proceeded to spill her story on Annie and Oige.

Despite the fact that experienced medics had never seen a cyst on a human heart, I was amazed at the number of people who had exactly the same condition as I had; or their brother had; or their friend. And just how eager they were to share the gory details. I learned to eschew those people like grease lightning.

Limited association

Prior to my health journey, I had a policy of never, ever, ever, ever ringing my mother before giving a motivational talk. The simple reason is that I'm paid good money to up-lift people and move them.

The mere thought however, of standing up in front of a group would traumatise my mother and fill her with terror. The trouble is – she'd inadvertently transfer that terror to me – lock, stock and smoking barrel. It's only natural for a mother to worry. Were I to ring her before a gig she'd be vividly aware of everything that could go wrong and ask each and everyone of the following questions.

'What happens if no one shows up?' (It's happened)

'What happens if too many people show up and there's not enough chairs and the room gets too stuffy?' (It's happened and I love it)

'What happens if the projector doesn't work?' (My best presentations of all time have been without one single overhead slide)

'What happens if you forget your lines?' (I do all the time and you know what! The audience rarely cop it)

Once the presentation is over, and whatever the outcome, I almost always ring my mother. We shoot the breeze on who was there, what they thought, what I'd do differently if I was doing it again. That's limited association and everyone's a winner.

I employed the same policy during my illness. There were things that needed sharing and much that wasn't.

Expanded association

There are some people who can uplift you even just by thinking about them. They should be the first entries in the 'Strengths' section of every SWOT Analysis. Make it your number one priority to spend more time with them. They will grow you more than any university education ever will. In the words of Rohn: 'Don't join an easy crowd. Go where the challenge is great and the emotions are high. Go where the expectations are so strong that they provoke you, push you and urgently insist that you not remain in one place. That way, you will grow and change.'

Some people just have it. They uplift you. And they are particularly valuable when you're mentally challenged. I recall with the greatest joy so many funny, invigorating and inspiring moments during those torrid times.

I still laugh remembering my friend Don Colleran who'd visit me once a week and fill me in on the gossip around town. I'd dump on him and he'd give me his response. One day I was complaining about the fact that my Medical Health Insurance Company insisted I stay in hospital to receive my antibiotics intravenously.

'I mean it just doesn't make sense Don.' I remonstrated.

'It costs a thousand euros per night to have me here whereas all I need is a qualified nurse to administer the drugs twice a day at home.'

'I know one.' Said Don enthusiastically.

'You know who.' I replied.

'I know a qualified nurse who'll do just that for half the price. In fact, she'll even sleep with you for that.'

I could be heard laughing all through the canteen.

On another day, he texted all his contacts to say that the medics had had a breakthrough. 'They've discovered that Ó Máille hasn't an infection at all. He's actually pregnant.'

Even the consultants laughed at this.

On one other occasion, whilst very sick in the Blackrock Clinic, my great friend Mary Anderson insisted on taking me out to lunch.

My CRPs (infection markers) had been over a 100 that morning and my renal function had drifted out to 1.3. I was clinically not a well man.

Yet, within as little as ten minutes, at Mary's special table in Roly's, and in her wonderful company, I'd forgotten utterly about my ailments and laughed my way through five excellent courses of lunch.

That evening I should have been exhausted from my exertions and most probably should have slept and recovered. I would have too, had I not been visited upon by four of my son's friends working in Dublin. I shared with them a porter cake that Mary A had given me that afternoon and the craic was mighty. On three separate occasions, the nurses asked us to quieten things down and eventually encouraged the lads to depart at 10 pm.

I was on the cusp of the deepest sleep when the door opened gently and in the darkness I heard a voice enquire.

'Paddy. Where's the light. I need you to review a book for me?'

It was my old school friend, Brendan Phelan, and he'd successfully eluded security by entering the clinic as the young lads were departing. He'd been asked to implement a management programme at work called 'The 4 Disciplines of Execution' and he was hoping I'd read the book for him and summarise it. As it transpired, I'd been meaning to study that book for years, and now, I didn't even have to buy it. What a win/win?

The following morning, I had my bloods taken by the phlebotomist at 7 am and the consultant arrived at 8.30 am to deliver the prognosis. I dreaded these consultations as invariably they had been negative most of the time.

'Pádraic, I can't rightly explain it, but your CRP levels this morning are down to 25 and you're renal function is back in at 1.1.'

He may have had difficulty explaining it, but I could. I'd been around some truly uplifting people the previous day.

In 'From Good to Great' Jim Collins discovered that all the great organisations had firstly gotten the right people on the bus. They had paradoxically done this prior to creating a vision or a BHAG. In addition, they were very rigorous about getting the wrong people off the bus. And when they had achieved those objectives, they aligned those people in the right positions on the bus.

Chapter 13
Befriend Failure

'I've missed more than 9000 shots in my life. I've lost more than 300 games. 26 times I've been trusted to take the game winning shot and I've missed. I've failed over and over and over again in my life. And that is why I succeed.'

Michael Jordan
The greatest basketball player of all time

Failure is greatly underrated.

From an early age, we are programmed to view it as something negative, odious and to be avoided at all costs. By our early teens, we have developed a near pathological aversion to it and our every decision is predicated upon grounds of safety, security and predictability.

As a consequence, we realise but a fraction of our potential. In our misguided efforts to play it safe, we eschew invaluable opportunities to grow, develop and flourish. Too late in the day, we appreciate the innate wisdom of that wonderful lady Helen Keller when she said 'Security does not exist in nature, nor do the children of men as a whole experience it … . Avoiding danger is no safer in the long run than outright exposure … Life is either a daring adventure or nothing.'

It is fortuitous therefore that young babies are as yet immune to the fear of failure. Otherwise they'd never learn to walk, talk or tie their shoes.

All success is characterised by layer upon layer of failure. Every outstanding person from Michael Jordan to Thomas Edison is a testament to the power of failure.

In a series of articles I published in the Galway Advertiser titled 'Conversations with Achievers', it emerged that failure had preceded success in the lives of every achiever I spoke with. In fact, the title of the articles could equally have been titled 'Conversations with Failures.' The only difference was that these people embraced failure as an inevitable component of the journey to success, and used it as a welcome catalyst to bigger and better opportunities. Rather than being discouraged by failure, it appears the 'Achiever' is possessed of a shred of DNA that sees them welcome failure as an opportunity to learn and persist through any number of temporary setbacks.

The definitive treatment for me however, on the power of failure is contained in the commencement address given by JK Rowling at the Annual Meeting of the Harvard Alumni Association titled "The Fringe Benefits of Failure and the Importance of Imagination.'

In it she describes that a mere seven years after graduating, she 'had failed on an epic scale.' 'An exceptionally short lived marriage had imploded, and I was jobless, a lone parent and as poor as it is possible to be in modern

Britain without being homeless. The fears my parents had had for me, and that I had had for myself, had both come to pass and by every usual standard, I was the biggest failure I knew.'

It is only in the desolate throes of failure that its potent power is unleashed.

I believe her address should be prescribed reading for every student returning to school or university in September because failure gave her that 'inner security that I had never attained by passing examinations.'

It should be promulgated from every pulpit in our churches because as she says 'You will never truly know yourself or the strength of your relationships, until both have been tested by adversity.'

Let us dispense therefore from the traditional perception of failure as being something 'negative, odious and to be avoided at all costs.' Rather, let us enthusiastically and intimately reframe it as part of the process of being alive and a necessary, inevitable and vital stepping stone on the journey to achievement, accomplishment and success.

Let us regard it as an opportunity to learn and grow and develop. An opportunity to expand our comfort zones and realise infinitely more of our true potential. A temporary setback that will induct us in the attitude, knowledge and skills required to triumph at exalted levels. An opportunity to live life on the edge and to enjoy the journey. An event that has been sent to serve us as opposed to obstruct us.

Some years ago, John Quinn interviewed Tony O'Reilly on his wonderful radio series 'The Open Mind.' The interview was replete with detail after detail on O'Reilly's no mean achievements in life, business and sport. As the interview drew to a close, Quinn enquired of O'Reilly if he'd ever overtly failed in his life.

O'Reilly described in vivid detail the events of a hotly contested Leinster Schools Senior Cup rugby final where he captained Old Belvedere against a highly fancied Blackrock College team. Late on in the game 'Belvo' were leading only to concede a late try to Blackrock to level the game. As the Blackrock place kicker was about to take the conversion, and ultimately decide the fate of the entire competition, O'Reilly was reminded of the only words of advice his father had given him prior to the game. 'Display grace under pressure at all times.'

With that, he walked up to the kicker, shook his hand and wished him well. As O'Reilly retreated, the Blackrock kicker duly converted the try leaving Old Belvedere the losers and O'Reilly feeling and looking like a wuss.

Twenty-seven years later, as Chairman of the Heinz Empire, O'Reilly again came under severe pressure. A Heinz product had to be recalled and the only people who could save Heinz from massive destruction was their arch rival – Del Monte.

O'Reilly approached the owner of Del Monte with little or no confidence for a successful outcome. To his amazement 'the man from Del Monte said Yes'.

It transpired that 'the man from Del Monte' was a practicing catholic whose local parish priest was an Irishman. When Del Monte enquired of him what he thought of O'Reilly, The priests reply was 'I know very little about him except that many years ago I saw him display great sportsmanship in difficult and losing circumstances.'

It demonstrates very clearly that sometimes, even when you lose, you win. Provided that is, that you stay in the game. The implications for success in any field therefore are threefold:

1. Get into the game. Sadly many of us are so paralysed by the fear of failure that we never even get started.
2. Stay in the game realising that you will inevitably encounter failure at every step of the way but that viewing failure as your friend as opposed to your foe is the surest route to success. As Thomas Watson, the founder of IBM said 'To succeed more, double your failure rate.' (Quote this to all parents, teachers, bank managers, bosses and whoever else is concerned about your present performance.)
3. Enjoy the game. The destination is not nearly as important as enjoying the journey.

Pádraig Ó Céidigh is the Chairman of the Adjudicating Committee of the Ernst Young Entrepreneur of the Year.

As such, he has interviewed hundreds of entrepreneurs globally and understands the mindset of an entrepreneur better than most. He makes some interesting comments about their attitude to failure.

'Their bottom line is not whether they succeed or fail. Neither is it about becoming the richest person in their country. It's about going into uncharted waters and trying something new. Certainty is a boring word for entrepreneurs. They embrace the beauty of uncertainty in every moment of their existence. With them, the only failure is not trying.'

I too have been visited by the failure spectre many times over the past six months. I know intimately the sinking feeling that I've failed my family, my customers and many other suppliers. I've taken massive comfort from that line.

EMBRACE THE BEAUTY OF UNCERTAINTY IN
EVERY MOMENT OF YOUR EXISTENCE

Don't quit

When things go wrong, as they sometimes will,
When the road you're trudging seems all uphill,
When the funds are low and the debts are high,
And you want to smile, but you have to sigh,
When care is pressing you down a bit,
Rest, if you must, but don't you quit.
Life is queer with its twists and turns,
As every one of us sometimes learns,
And many a failure turns about,
When he might have won had he stuck it out;
Don't give up though the pace seems slow —
You may succeed with another blow.
Often the goal is nearer than,
It seems to a faint and faltering man,
Often the struggler has given up,
When he might have captured the victor's cup,
And he learned too late when the night slipped down,
How close he was to the golden crown.
Success is failure turned inside out —
The silver tint of the clouds of doubt,
And you never can tell how close you are,
It may be near when it seems so far,
So stick to the fight when you're hardest hit —
It's when things seem worst that you must not quit.

Author unknown

Chapter 14
The Big Yellow Bastard

Neither of us would probably ever have bought her had we known what she was called.

And no bride on her wedding night was ever lavished with such reverence as he did when extolling her every component.

He'd installed new timing belts in each of the two engines after one year even though the industry standard was happy with one in five. He'd applied three veneers of yellow protective paint coating to protect the rubber tubes from abrasion – 'just to be sure'. When he lovingly insisted I feel for myself the quality of 'the two new nipples he'd fitted on the impellers to enable manual freshwater cleaning' it took me a tad to deck he wasn't joking.

'Ask him how fast she goes and how she planes over big waves' urged Shane impatiently.

I politely doused my teenage sons ardour by explaining to him that Mr. Smith was an Englishman and that the English care for their boats in the same manner as they do their cars.

'Ask him so what the name means. I hate ponsy French names on boats'.

When I did ask however, as to what the name 'El Cabron Amarillo' meant, Mr. Smith was for once less than assured. 'Can't help you that mate. I bought it in Spain from a chap who said the name had something to do with her ability to perform in rough weather. As both my wife and I got sea sick the first time we took her out, we never really used it much since.'

I was tempted to remind him of Seneca when he said that 'boats are safe enough in the harbour but that's not what they were made for' but thought better of it.

Her identity, and reputation, were quickly revealed on her maiden voyage from New Quay in County Clare on a blustery force seven westerly wind coming straight off a 3000 mile fetch of angry Atlantic ocean. Little five year old Ivan Brophy had just returned from a year in Spain where his mother Joanne had been teaching Spanish to the Spaniards. Upon seeing the boat's name he erupted into laughter. 'Cool name Pádraic!'

'What's so funny about it? I enquired suspiciously.

Eyeing up the other boats in the harbour, he proceeded to rattle off their names.

'All the other boats here are named after cissies. There's the 'Lady Mary' and 'The LE Orla' and 'The Queen of Connemara'. Yours, on the other hand, is a real man's name.'

'What does it mean? I demanded impatiently.

'The Big Yellow Bastard' he proclaimed in awe and respect.

And so she was. Over the years, she'd taken just about everything the Atlantic had thrown at her. Wide at the stern, deep at the bow and propelled by two faithful Honda 90s she'd more than paid her fare.

Which was more than could be said for the way I cared for her. All this year I had left her moored in the turbulent waters of New Quay. I was always too busy to take her out and rest her up for the winter. In short, I simply hadn't cared? And the wear and tear had inexorably begun to take their toll. The hull, perforated by the constant attrition of the rocky New Quay seabed, was leaking slowly.

Not enough to prevent me going to Inis Oirr one fine Wednesday in April. All that week, windguru.com had been forecasting almost perfect calm conditions for Wednesday. As long as the delicate bilge pumps kept working I'd be fine. And they did. And, as always when I set foot on Inis Oirr, my heart soared.

I legged it out past the white beach bounded by turquoise green water and paused for a sos (break) at the wreck of the Plessey. From there I went off piste as far west as you can go on this continent and then back by the tail of Inis Meain – and was back at the harbour in under 90 minutes.

Just as well too, as the transom of the heavily flooded boat was less than one inch above the water line. I began baling with purpose. As the engine shafts resurfaced I couldn't help noticing what were the remnants of Mr. Smith's pristine nipples. They were now rusted over and covered in green slime. I shuddered to think what he'd have made of his boat had he seen her now.

Telepathically I heard a voice booming down at me from the harbour wall.

'Bail ó Dhia ar an obair ach nach trua é an fallaí'. (God bless the work but what a pity about the neglect).

It was part blessing, and part admonishment. And because it had been administered by one Sean Bartley, it stung.

I had first met Sean Bartley (Old Bartley) more than 30 years ago, when as a wayward young student from university he'd tried to put some Smácht on me. Now in his late 80s, he'd not left this tiny island more than a dozen times, and only then to venture as far as one of the other Aran Islands or to Galway. He still wore traditional breidín trousers held up with a multicoloured críos and topped with a báinín waistcoat.

We consulted over pints of chilled porter in Tigh Ned's. There was no end to Sean Bartley's wisdom.

'Do you see that reef off Gregory's sound? he asked me pointing to a vicious looking archipelago of rocks to the north of the island. 'I was fishing lobsters there many years ago with one of my sons when we clipped a rock and holed the currach. My son began to bale furiously and managed to keep the boat afloat. The only thing was, we weren't going anywhere. And these were days long before mobile phones or two way radios, or even life jackets for that matter.

'With darkness falling, and the weather deteriorating, what would you have done Pádraiceen?'

Sean Bartley, like Socrates before him, understood the massive power of questions. And like Socrates, he sat back, and I have no doubt would have waited all day if needs be for me to answer.

Aware that currachs are made from stretched tarred canvas, I knew that they could be plugged. 'I'd have taken my shirt off, plugged the hole and rowed like the clappers to dry land. And after that I'd have got the best currach builder on the island to repair it as good as new'.

'Maith thú a bhuachaill' (good man) he said warmly.

'And that's the secret to a happy life. Spend part of your time baling and part of your time rowing and another part of your time mending the leaks. Take care in particular to mend any leaks in your most important possessions such as your boat, your nets and your home. Faillí (neglect) is the greatest curse known to man and is the cause of most hardship in life. And speaking of leaks, its time you were heading back to the mainland'.

As I powered the RIB back towards Black Head and on in by Gleninagh and Ballyvaughan Bay, I was, as always after a session with Sean Bartley, assailed by a BFO – a Blinding Flash of the Obvious.

Neglect. It is the Big Yellow Bastard.

Because every second, of every minute, of every hour, of every day – a war rages deep within us.

Beckoning loudest, is the call to *create*. To *be* more. To *do* more. To *have* more.

To write a book. To raise a great family. To create an amazing lifestyle.

In short, to create the freedom that allows us to do what we want, when we want, where we want, with whom we want.

Our deepest instinct is to pursue that calling with all our resolve. To revel in the learning of setbacks. To exalt in the triumph of success. To bask in the fulfilment of helping others.

Yet that big yellow bastard stalks us every step of the way.

For the most part, we're blissfully unaware of his scheming presence. At other times we'll be seduced utterly by his ineffable charm and instant gratification from all things appearing odious.

Do not be deluded by his innocent and demure aura. It's invidious at best and toxic at worst.

'How do I recognise him? I hear you say.

You'll recognise him as the one who questions who the hell you think you are to dream big. Who tempts you lasciviously to put things off for another minute, hour, day – lifetime. Who starts out as a sniffle and then develops into a disease – the most vile disease in all humanity. A virulent scourge that defies the most potent of antibiotics.

He's big, he's yellow, he's a bastard and when he grips you, he's harder to kick than crack cocaine.

He's called 'Neglect' and he's all pervasive.

'Neglect' derives from the Latin *'neglegere'* which literally means to make light of. Inexorably, we begin to make light of those possessions Bartley waxed so lyrically about. We begin to neglect our:

Bodies: a third of all Americans are obese (making light of their weight)

Customers: 68% of all customers we lose is due to apathy – we neglected to care for them.

Relationships: 50% of marriages now end up in divorce – once again, neglect is a prime player.

Life's calling: How often do we witness talented, educated, privileged people neglect what they'd really love to do.

Neglecting our calling is life's greatest travesty.

It's the reason we've rock stars who don't rock and entrepreneurs who never start a business and sports people who never kick a ball.

But Bono and Michael O'Leary and even Brian O'Driscoll himself – were also seduced by neglect. They too heard the clarion call of mañana and mediocrity and missed opportunity. They managed to keep their trousers on however.

What they understood is that doing is not the hard part. Getting started is. And the panacea to getting started is that great Irish mindset called Smácht. It means discipline. And it's the perfect antidote to Faillí or Neglect.

The scribe who penned the following lines understood implicitly the significance of the phrase 'El Cabron Amarillo'.

For want of a nail the shoe was lost.
For want of a shoe the horse was lost.
For want of a horse the rider was lost.
For want of a rider the message was lost.
For want of a message the battle was lost.

For want of a battle the kingdom was lost.
And all for the want of a horseshoe nail.

My first call when I arrived safely back to New Quay was to Frank Byrnes Autobody Repairs. It felt good.

When we lose our health or our income or anything, for that matter, it's useful to examine those areas we've been neglecting.

In my case, I quickly became aware that I'd worked myself to a frazzle over the past twenty five years. I'd neglected the signs of sore throats, night sweats and irregular palpitations. Similarly, from a business perspective, I'd neglected to embrace the vast opportunity that the Internet presents. I'd been too busy being busy.

Now, I have the present moment. And some discipline. And a great SHAG.

Chapter 15
The Ultimate Time Management Tool

Do you mean now?' Yogi Berra replied, when asked for the time.

I was due to deliver the course in twenty minutes time, and not alone was I late, I was lost.

It's highly unprofessional, and even disrespectful, to arrive late to any course, but when it's on Time Management and you're the presenter, it adds considerably to the dilemma.

I'd had my excuses. The kids chose last night to nurture tummy bugs and weren't in the slightest bit sympathetic to my early start. There were road works in Limerick which held me up for twenty minutes. They'd even changed the signage for Kilmallock.

But the real reason I was late was because I'd started out late. It was lesson no. 1 in all our courses.

YOU ARE RESPONSIBLE 100% FOR YOUR RESULTS IN LIFE

I had three choices. One, I had an AA road map and I could consult it. Two, I had a mobile phone and I could ring the client and ask for directions. Three, I could ask someone on the road for directions.

I did none of the above. I continued driving. And not alone did I continue driving, I put the boot down and drove like the hammers of hell.

And sure enough, in exactly twenty minutes I arrived. In Charleville. Eight miles to the west of Kilmallock.

I did what I should have done in the first place. I rang my client, Caroline Boles from Senator Engineering, and I gave her a skin full of excuses. She listened attentively.

'Where are you now?' She asked helpfully.

'I'm in Charleville.'

'Where precisely in Charleville?

'I'm outside a fire station.'

'Perfect. You turn around. Take the next turn right at the hotel. Continue straight on for three miles. At O'Neills pub take a left for Kilmallock. It's signposted all the way from there. Now repeat that for me.'

'Super.' She said. 'You'll be here in fifteen minutes and we can start the course at ten.'

And then came the game changer.

'Pádraic, there's no point going faster if you're going in the wrong direction.'

The foregoing ditty lays bare the first two principles of effective time management. Firstly, know where you're going or as Stephen Covey so practically put it 'Begin with the end in mind.' And if you've the slightest doubt about your destination, consult a map or stop and get directions.

And the second principle is to know exactly where you are in relation to your destination or as Jim Collins describes it. 'Confront the brutal facts.'

The trouble is we have exams to pass and kids to raise and mortgages to pay and before we know it we get busy. Manically busy. And the coordinates of those guiding principles become fudged and opaque and clouded. And we unconsciously become subsumed with the rest of the world in a frenetic cycle of 'doing, doing, doing.' It becomes our drug of choice and we become hopelessly addicted to 'doing without thinking.' And as Henry Ford commented. 'Thinking is the hardest work there is, which is probably the reason why so few engage in it.'

Although I had mentored the good and the great on the theory of these issues with a modicum of success I had much in common with the cobbler's child or the smoking doctor or the fat personal trainer. As they say in the university of life. 'In theory there is no difference between theory and practice. In practice there is.'

One of the most powerful benefits of getting sick was that it enabled me to take time to reflect more deeply on what I wanted in life, and paradoxically, on what I didn't want ever again.

A recurring theme in many of my medical consultations was the level of worry and stress and pressure that I'd inadvertently built into my life over the years. I deliver high intensity training sessions to groups of people and I had come to crave the buzz and challenge and adulation of a great gig. What had gone unnoticed to me was that I was doing five of these gigs a week, week in week out, for the past number of years. And whilst I was addicted to the adrenalin rush of these sessions, each and everyone of them was a live show and brought with it a corresponding measure of worrying about what would happen if it went wrong or I wasn't perfect every performance.

It's the dilemma of addicts the world over. How do you get the hit without suffering the hangover. I passionately wanted to continue delivering material that motivates and inspires and educates. But without the physical and mental wear and tear that had nigh killed me.

I'm a great believer in the power of questions to help reframe a situation or predicament. And a question I'd helped many clients achieve breakthroughs with in the past was. 'What's the opposite to what you're currently experiencing?'

'What's the opposite of worry and stress?' I asked myself one morning starting my walk out the Flaggy Shore.

Unlike mobile phone technology, the Divine WiFi or universal intelligence has a different means of responding to requests. It's best accessed in quietness or nature or whilst doing something physical. I had the perfect reception and signal.

'POM' It whispered gently and reassuringly.

That's the thing about the Divine WiFi. It rarely ever gives you the answer on a plate but revels in riddles and metaphors and acronyms. I'd learned over the years to remain patient and playful and persistent with it as the answer is invariably the right one, when it arrives.

'POM' are clearly my initials and also the acronym I shared with you earlier called 'Poor Old Me.' But how was 'POM' the opposite of worry and stress and tension?

I recalled vividly a paragraph I'd read in an excellent book by Brian Tracy called *Maximum Achievement*. In it, he counselled that we should all make 'Peace of Mind' our ultimate priority.

And there I had it.

'Peace of Mind.'

A new SHAG. A new direction. A new destination. A new philosophy.

From that moment on I resolved to make massive use of the question. 'What are the things that contribute to my POM and what are those things that detract from my POM.'

But what about the second principle of effective time management, namely current reality. Where was I now in relation to POM?

The reality was that I was on a different planet in many respects. I had an infection that continued to defy medical explanation and ominously I lacked the energy and drive to generate an income the way I used to. The banks had given me a short reprieve on my financial obligations but that would come crashing down like a ton of bricks any-day now.

Imagine telling them my new strategic goal was 'POM!'

When the mind has two conflicting images, it uses cognitive dissonance or creative tension to remedy the issue. This is the process and bedrock of all change. When a lady sees a stunning outfit in a shop window and although she's as broke as a pauper, she will always experience creative tension.

One picture she'll screen is how thinner and younger and more seductive she'll look and feel in the outfit. She'll hear mildly envious comments from her friends on how stylish and attractive she is. And she'll begin to feel awesome.

The other picture however, is that her cards are all maxed out; she owes a plethora of bills; and she doesn't get paid 'til the end of the month.

And this is where creative tension kicks in. It will gravitate towards whichever picture is most vivid, dominant and clear. And if she opts to visualise herself feeling brilliant in the dress, her mind will emerge with all sorts of weird and wonderful solutions. She simply needs to put the picture out there and the answer will appear.

I did too that glorious December morning. I now knew I wanted POM but I also wanted to do the great work I had done in the past if that was possible. And I just love that quote from Zig Ziglar saying that 'Money's not the most important thing in the world but it ranks right up there with oxygen.' I wanted to make serious money and do great work without ever having to worry about money again.

I paused for a rest at the Martello Tower in Finavarra and gazed out past Ballyvaughan and Gleninagh towards Blackhead lighthouse. I thought of all the times it had guided me in from Aran and Connemara over the years and had prevented me going aground on the Burren rocks.

By the end of that walk I had three lighthouses to aim for in my life. Peace of Mind; Purpose; and Prosperity.

They needed further honing and toning. But that would come.

The third principle of effective time management is that the morning is the rudder of your day. The rudder is a lever and the time management literature abounds with references to the value of 'high leverage activities.' High leverage activities are those that generate a disproportion-ately higher return on your time investment. Examples from a management perspective would be taking time to plan; organise; delegate; inspect; train and build strong relationships.

At a self-management level, I have urged throughout this book the value of meditating first thing in the morning. It will quieten your mind and connect you to the source of all wisdom, insight and knowledge. You will approach problems and obstacles with a solutions-based approach that will effortlessly reveal solutions and answers 'out of the blue.' It will provide you with a sense of calm and con-trol that will pervade your engagements throughout the day.

In summary, you will be more focused, organised and connected.

During your period of meditation you can combine it with a period of guided visualisation to amplify the power of your SHAGs and goals. As mentioned repeatedly throughout the book, the subconscious mind is incapable of distinguishing between what is real and imagined. Spend a few minutes in quiet relaxation picturing the 'end in mind' of that day's meetings, activities, presentations and goals. And you can begin the day with those two high leverage activities before you get out of your warm cosy bed.

Move vigorously early in the morning. It will make you feel better, look better, think better, act better, earn better, perform better and love better. I can't think of a greater return on your investment of time.

Work is important in life. Quite apart from paying the bills, it gives us a sense of meaning and purpose and fulfilment and contribution. I only really experienced this for myself when I had 'no work.' It was a soul destroying space.

In his book *Do More Great Work,* Michael Bungay Stanier makes a distinction between three other types of work – bad work, good work and great work. Bad work is simply plain unproductive work that is characterised by no vision, poor planning, boring meetings, bureaucracy and a waste of time. Good work is the productive, day to day, necessary work that we do well. Great work, on the other hand, is the work that juices you where you're playing at your peak and in the zone. Great work is the stuff of impact and meaning and legacy. It's also the work that we love to do. It's that activity where time is suspended and our focus and engagement is total.

Sadly for many of us we spend most of our lives doing good work. It's safe, secure and comfortable. Voltaire said it first and then Jim Collins used it in the opening line of his iconic book. 'Good is the enemy of great.' The reason we don't have a great business or career or income is that we have a good one. Because going from good to great requires a sea change in our thinking and mindset and attitude.

But it's a change that all great time managers choose to make. Even if it does mean jettisoning the safe, pensionable and secure job. Steve Jobs knew full well the meaning of great work.

Your work is going to fill a large part of your life, and the only way to be truly satisfied is to do what you believe is great work. And the only way to do great work is to love what you do. If you haven't found it yet, keep looking. Don't settle. As with all matters of the heart, you'll know when you find it.

And one of the ways to do great work and love what you do is to create. When you're creating a baby (especially); a business; a career; a home; a painting; a song; a story – you're doing great work and doing what you love.

Most of all, create a legacy.

Unlike adolescents in many African tribes, my initiation to manhood occurred in the Palace Bar on Main Street Bundoran. My Uncle Michael, the Chief of the Clan, was taking my induction most seriously. The first pint involved a general discussion on the art of holding your drink. The second, a detailed strategy on how to beat the bookies most of the time. The third was a truncated version of the reproduction system. It addressed those aspects of the subject missing from the text book *Intermediate Biology*.

It was during the fourth pint that Uncle Michael proceeded to the career guidance module of the investiture.

'What do you want your legacy to be?' He asked seriously.

'What does a legacy mean?' I asked honestly.

'What do you want to be remembered as? An example or a warning?'

'That will be your legacy.'

Marianne Williamson sums up beautifully what a legacy is in her book *A Return to Love.*

> *Our deepest fear is not that we are inadequate. Our deepest fear is that we are powerful beyond measure. It is our light, not our darkness that most frightens us. We ask ourselves, 'Who am I to be brilliant, gorgeous, talented, fabulous?' Actually, who are you not to be? You are a child of God. Your playing small does not serve the world. There is nothing enlightened about shrinking so that other people won't feel insecure around you. We are all meant to shine, as children do. We were born to make manifest the glory of God that is within us. It's not just in some of us; it's in everyone. And as we let our own light shine, we unconsciously give other people permission to do the same. As we are liberated from our own fear, our presence automatically liberates others.*

There will always be pain and failure and setbacks in life. We can either moan about them or solve them. One of the characteristics of great time managers is that they have developed the habit of self-discipline. Elbert Hubbard defined self-discipline as 'the ability to do what you should do, when you should do it, whether you feel like it or not.' This requires delaying gratification in the short term in order to derive a greater reward in the longer term.

This is one of the other great tensions or games that constantly plays out in our minds. Let's call the two players Smácht and Faillí. Smácht is the Irish word for discipline – doing the right thing. Faillí is the Irish word for neglect – deferring activities we don't like to do until later. It's an insidious internal dialogue that if left uncontrolled will seriously sabotage your productivity and happiness.

A great habit to develop is to do those activities you don't feel like doing – first thing in the day. Make it part of your morning routine. It will develop your self-discipline muscle in such a way that it becomes habitual to do this. When this happens, watch your peace of mind and productivity and prosperity soar.

Think Buffalo. Buffalos instinctively charge head on into the storm as opposed to cattle who are programmed to run away from it. By heading into the storm early buffalos come out the other side quickly. The net result is that they minimise greatly their exposure to the adversity and turbulence of the storm. Cattle, on the other hand, are programmed to run with the wind and paradoxically maximise their exposure to it.

Like cattle, we spend an inordinate amount of time running away from painful situations. This is a pity because one of the truisms of life is that there's no gain without pain or what hurts instructs. Rory Vaden, in a cracking book called *Take the Stairs*, talks about 'the Pain Paradox.' He explains that we're continuously seduced by short-term pleasure at the expense of long-term pain. The giddy high of an extra marital affair or the instant buzz of a scatter of drinks all provide for intense short-term pleasure but at a massive cost. 'The great irony here is that what seems easy and feels good in the short term usually doesn't last long. The Pain Paradox of decision making states the short-term easy leads to the long-term difficult, while the short-term difficult leads to the long-term easy.'

Great time managers learn to suck up pain. They front up to problems and worries early and decisively. They understand intuitively that time spent on problem solving is infinitely more valuable than time spent avoiding problems and hoping they'll go away. As we've said before, hope is not a strategy.

There are a number of psychological zones that have a big impact on the quality of our results. Our comfort zone is safe and secure and can protect us along our journey. Our growth and development and mastery derive from our courage to reach out to the zone of continuous improvement – our stretch zone. This is not to be confused with your danger zone. Your stretch zone challenges you to play to your limits in every area of your life.

A great affirmation to repeat daily, preferably upon awakening and sleeping, is.

'I am constantly expanding my comfort zone.'

The fact that time management is the most in demand training course in the world tells you something of both the challenges that people face with respect to their time and also of its importance. I've pleasure in revealing that I have trained with and worked with many of the world thought leaders on the subject such as Dan Stamp, Peter Hancock, Stephen Covey, Brian Tracy, Tony Buzan and Tony Robbins. I've used and tried and researched every conceivable time management tool from Time Text to The Franklin Covey Planner to a plethora of electronic versions.

When you've completed all the courses, and listened to all the gurus and used all their systems, you'll realise that there is one ultimate time management tool that stands head and shoulders above the rest.

It's free, accessible now and it works perfectly.

It's called the Present Moment.

If you think about it, Louise Hay was on the money when she said 'The point of power is always in the present moment' because the present moment lived greatly and fully is the surest guarantee of a great and fulfilled future.

Chapter 16
Conclusion

Men occasionally stumble over the truth, but most of them pick themselves up and hurry off as if nothing had happened.

Winston Churchill

My Uncle Stíofáin was an avid sportsman and he never tired of relating the parable of the Moose.

Two hunters chartered a plane to take them deep into moose territory in Northern Canada. To their amazement and delight they succeeded in bagging six specimen moose.

As they were boarding the aircraft on the return journey the pilot refused to take two of the moose on the grounds that they exceeded the official weight restrictions for the light aircraft.

The hunters were furious.

'Last year we also shot six moose and the pilot had no problem taking them on board and he had exactly the same plane as yours.'

The tirade might well have ended there but for the appearance of a hefty wad of green backs. Stíofáin always maintained that it really is the universal language.

Tragically, upon takeoff, the aircraft stuttered and shuddered with the excess overload and careered violently into the dense wilderness.

Miraculously, the two hunters survived unscathed from the crash. As they emerged from the burning wreckage one turned to the other and enquired.

'Any idea where we are?'

'Not exactly, but I think we're very close to where we crashed last year.'

I got very positive results from my blood tests last week. Thankfully the infection seems to have abated and after seven gruelling months of disease and despair I'm gradually regaining energy and strength.

My immediate response disappointingly, was not one of intense gratitude and joy and reflection but rather, how quickly could I return to work and make up for lost time and money.

I was rushing my recovery.

I was reminded of rule number two from Dr. Chérie Carter-Scott's magnificent 'The Ten Rules For Being Human.'

Rule Two – You will be presented with lessons.
You are enrolled in a full-time informal school called 'life'.
Each day in this school you will have the opportunity to learn
lessons. You may like the lessons or hate them, but you have
designed them as part of your curriculum.

What wonderful wisdom!

I have always sensed that the experiences and events of life happen for a reason and that that reason is beneficial for us.

I had just experienced a sequence of health episodes that were rarer than rocking horse shit and like the Moose hunters I too was about to proceed without learning the lesson.

But what was the lesson?

Only yesterday I was talking with Joe Connolly, the legendary Galway hurler, and he shared with me some advice his father had once given him. He had once counselled Joe that when you find yourself in times of trouble, 'Tabhair am dó.' (Give it time).

G.I.T. for short.

That's the prescription to solve all your problems. To have the Smácht (self-discipline) to give all your problems time.

That won't be easy. I'll tell you why.

Modern marketing, of which I profess to be a graduate, is programming you overtly and subliminally every second of the day to taking the easy way out; the short cut; the quick fix.

Think about it. You can now lose a stone in a week. You can find the love of your life in a weekend. And with a deposit of as little as ten percent you can own a new house for life in a day.

The emphasis is on easy, short and quick.

The reality is disease, divorce and debt.

The facts are that two thirds of our population are over-weight with almost one third obese. Nearly one in every two marriages breaks up irretrievably. Only 5% of the population will be financially rich at the age of 65 with 54% being broke and relying on others to support them.

In order to live a healthy and happy and abundant life, it is necessary to cultivate Smácht in abundance. Smácht is not just the Irish word for discipline. It is an attitude, a way of living and working, and a habit.

Regrettably, the notion of self-discipline has endured a cynical press and we have been poorly trained in the benefits of Smácht. There's a misconception that self-discipline is a prison whereas in actuality it's the key to freedom.

Jim Rohn summarised it wonderfully when he said.

We must all suffer from one of two pains: the pain of discipline or the pain of regret. The difference is discipline weighs ounces while regret weighs tons.

Our education system – students and teachers alike – have often been faulted with our attitude towards self-discipline. Our concluding story illustrates this magically.

A client of ours went to wake his son up the first morning back after the Christmas break.

'Wake up son, it's time for school.' The Dad said enthusiastically.

'I'm not going to school today.' The son replied stubbornly.

'Have you a good reason why?' The Dad responded reasonably.

'I have three reasons why. Firstly, I hate school. Secondly, the students are always slagging me. And thirdly, the teachers have no interest.' The son argued defiantly.

'Now here are three reasons why you'll get your butt out of bed pronto.' Said the Dad assertively.

'Firstly, it's your responsibility. Secondly, you're 42 years of age. And thirdly, you're the Headmaster.'

You too are responsible for your results in life and the legacy you create. And it doesn't matter whether you're 12 or

42 or 92, the issue isn't age, it's maturity. And you're the Boss.

MAY YOUR YEAR BE FILLED WITH **PEACE** AND **PURPOSE** AND **PROSPERITY.**

BEGIN BY HONOURING
THE MORNING
FOR IT IS THE RUDDER
OF YOUR DAY.

TAKE TIME TO BE
STILL AND LISTEN
TO YOUR QUIET INNER VOICE.

MOVE YOUR BODY # VIGOROUSLY.
YOU WILL FEEL BETTER. LOOK BETTER. THINK BETTER. ACT BETTER. EARN BETTER. LOVE BETTER. PERFORM BETTER. THERE IS NO GREATER RETURN ON ANY INVESTMENT.

YOU ARE HAPPIEST WHEN YOU ARE
CREATING
BEGIN THIS MOMENT TO CREATE.
A BABY. A BUSINESS. A CAREER.
A PAINTING. A SONG. A STORY.

BUT MOST OF ALL
CREATE A LEGACY

BE REMEMBERED AS AN EXAMPLE NOT AS A WARNING.

DISCOVER AT ALL COSTS WHAT **YOU LOVE** TO DO
AND DO IT # GREATLY & PASSIONATELY
EVEN IF THIS MEANS JETTISONING YOUR SECURE JOB.

RESOLVE THIS YEAR TO LIVE LIFE LIKE A
BUFFALO CHARGING
HEAD ON INTO YOUR WORRIES & FEARS THEREBY MINIMISING YOUR EXPOSURE TO ADVERSITY

TRAVEL EXTENSIVELY
NOT JUST GEOGRAPHICALLY
BUT TO THE EDGES AND FRONTIERS OF YOUR COMFORT ZONES. THERE, YOU'LL FIND
YOUR AND # PEACE PURPOSE AND PROSPERITY

ENJOY THE JOURNEY... IT IS MORE IMPORTANT THAN THE DESTINATION.

MOSTLY TODAY **BE GRATEFUL** FOR THIS MOMENT.

WHEN YOU'VE COMPLETED ALL THE COURSES YOU'LL REALISE THAT IT IS **THE ULTIMATE TIME MANAGEMENT TOOL.**

P.S. - ALWAYS FIND THE BEST IN EVERY PERSON AND SITUATION AND MOSTLY IN YOURSELF. IT'LL SAVE YOU BUCKETS OF TIME.

THE PRESENT MOMENT.

The Ultimate Time Management Tool © 2015
By Pádraic Ó Máille - The Smácht Guy
www.omaille.ie | Email: p@omaille.ie

Acknowledgements

You are the average of the five people you are surrounded by most of the time.

Jim Rohn

This book would not exist without my wife Annie. Neither would I.

I recall two weeks after my operation meeting the musician Garry Ó'Briain, who'd had a liver transplant a year prior to my operation. He explained to me that he'd had to undergo a rigorous interview process prior to becoming eligible for a liver transplant and that the first component of it was the existence of a strong and supportive and loving relationship. You simply cannot 'get on the bus' without it because it has been proven that those with a stable and loving relationship have a far higher probability of surviving and thriving an illness or trauma.

I mightn't have secured an 'A' in my cardiac MRI but what I lacked there I more than compensated for with the unconditional love and support I got from Annie. As the kids used to say 'you'd swear she'd undergone the operation herself' such was the pain and stress she endured with me.

As for the kids – Shane, Sarah, Harry and Oige – they matured into adults overnight. They sat stoically through some of the grim medical meetings where the various risks were discussed in raw and naked detail. They asked hard questions which would have been much easier to eschew. Most of all, they provided a comfort and security that no book could ever produce.

Liam Ryan, who sat in the back row of 6A with me and who'd survived the most terminal of cancers fourteen years ago, gave me some great advice on being a patient and dealing with the medics. 'Be the best patient you can be and remember that although you may not think it at the time, the medics actually do see the bigger picture. If they request that you do something, however unpalatable, say 'Yes Doctor. I'll do it, now.'

I cannot praise the medical profession highly enough.

My immediate medical team were outstanding, not just in terms of clinical competence but in their care and compassion. They were accessible, responsive and empathetic seven days a week. Although I had consultations with at least twelve different consultants, I would like to pay particular tribute to my own GP Barbara O'Beirne and to Jonathan Lyne and Lars Nolke in the Blackrock Clinic.

Some other doctors had significant inputs into this book also. Paddy O'Malley, consultant urologist in the Galway Clinic, and a good friend but no relation, provided me with the phrase 'as rare as rocking horse shit' which I'd never heard before. Pat Harrold, a GP in Nenagh and easily one of Ireland's finest writers and an old university buddy, truncated the title accordingly and edited the manuscript. Dr Dílis Clare, a former Smáchter, who kept me pumped up with the finest of herbs to charge my depleting energies.

My cousin Joey Costello, an anaesthetist in Galway, interpreted 'medicalese' for me and provided me with just enough information to keep me informed yet not paranoid. He is blessed with DNA that combines his father's clinical competence with his mother's care and compassion.

Although an orthopaedic surgeon professionally, it's as a visionary that I pay tribute to Jimmy Sheehan, founder of the Blackrock and Galway Clinics. If Carlsberg were to do hospitals they'd do both these clinics. The level of accommodation and comfort matches that of a 5 star hotel and the level of patient care rivals that of Disney.

I took clinical competence as a given. I was blown away by the quality of patient service and care. In particular, I single out the front of house people. On one occasion, when the infection had resurged uninvited yet again, I rang my consultant's suite and apologised to his secretary for hassling him again.

'Don't you be one bit apologetic Pádraic. That's what we're here for.'

That type of willingness to serve and care for the patient pervaded every level of both clinics from Margaret and

Irene at reception in the Galway Clinic to Fr. Gerry, the ultimate front of house person in the Blackrock Clinic.

On another occasion, Annie dragged me kicking and screaming back to A&E in the Galway Clinic with a roasting temperature and severe pain. Within 14 minutes of entry I was seen by a doctor and within the next 90 minutes I was on a drip in a private room. This is incredible responsiveness and sublime patient care.

Jimmy Sheehan once told me that as a young boy his passion was to become a carpenter – that he loved to create and make things. To this end he has succeeded in spades.

I've argued strongly in the book that 'attitude is more important than fact.' Thank you sincerely to all those people who uplifted my spirits.

I've often commented that, in my experience, nurses and teachers make for great business people and now I'm not surprised why. Grace Murphy in the Blackrock Clinic and Nessa Gillen in the Galway Clinic were supremely organised, focused and efficient. They were tender and tough in equal measure and provided us with much confidence and reassurance.

To former teachers Brendan O'Rourke, who reminded me that Smácht was all I needed, and to Padraig Ó Céidigh, who smuggled me out to that infamous Ernst Young function in Citywest, míle buíochas.

Sincere thanks to Toni and David Simpson, who so graciously provided the most hospitable and welcoming refuge whilst Annie and the kids were in Dublin. And to the best neighbours in the world, the Sweeney's of New Quay, who so kindly looked after Potter, the dog, when we were away.

Thank you to my great friend David Tarpey who not only taught me to live more in the present moment but is such a shining example of how to do it.

Thank you to Lorna O'Brien of Author Serve in New Quay who did a wonderful job typesetting and producing this book. And to Janine Sullivan of JK Sullivan Design who has designed such a marvellous cover.

Thank you to the Smácht community who showered me with good wishes and messages of positivity. In particular thanks to the members of Smácht Ór in Galway. They nudged me to have a S.H.A.G. when it was the farthest thing from my mind. They reminded me of the power of Smácht when I'd lost hope in it myself. And they asked hard questions when it was infinitely easier to avoid asking them. More than anything else they prove the power of a support or mastermind group, the core ethos of Smácht.

Finally, thank you to all those of you who responded to my blog posts and encouraged me to publish it in book format. That Smácht and purpose and focus was what got me through the very low times.

And as Mark Twain once famously said. 'I can live for three whole months on one compliment.' I can too. If this book has helped you please connect with me on p@omaille.ie

Helpful Reading

Anam Chara. John O'Donohue
Anatomy of an Illness. Norman Cousins
A Return to Love. Marianne Williamson
Awaken the Giant Within. Tony Robbins
Conversations with God. Neale Donald Walsch
Do More Great Work. Michael Bungay Stanier
Eat that Frog. Brian Tracy
First Things First. Stephen Covey
Five Major Pieces to the Life Puzzle. Jim Rohn
From Good to Great. Jim Collins
Getting Things Done. David Allen
Getting Well Again. O. Carl Simonton, MD
Great by Choice. Jim Collins
How to Stop Worrying and Start Living. Dale Carnegie
How to Win Friends and Influence People. Dale Carnegie
If Life is a Game, These are the Rules. Dr. Chérie Carter-Scott
Maximum Achievement. Brian Tracy
Take the Stairs. Rory Vaden
Think and Grow Rich. Napoleon Hill
The 4 Disciplines of Execution. McChesney, Covey and Huling.
The Midas Power. Pádraic Ó Máille
The New Psycho-Cybernetics. Maxwell Maltz, MD
The Power of Positive Thinking. Norman Vincent Peale
The Power of Your Subconscious Mind. Dr. Joseph Murphy
The Road Less Travelled. M. Scott Peck
The Seasons of Life. Jim Rohn
The Seven Habits of Highly Effective People. Stephen Covey
The Seven Spiritual Laws of Success. Deepak Chopra
The Strangest Secret. Earl Nightingale
Unlimited Power. Tony Robbins
Who Moved My Cheese? Spencer Johnson

About the Author

Pádraic Ó Máille is a popular speaker, trainer and writer and is the creator of Smácht, a training and consultancy business. He has helped thousands of people to realise more of their potential through one simple message. This core message is that Smácht, the Irish word for discipline, is the ultimate key to all accomplishment.

'Smácht means creating the self-discipline needed to getting ourselves doing the right things simply because they're right. This will frequently involve doing things we'd prefer not to be doing. But once Smácht becomes an ingrained habit, your success in every endeavour is virtually guaranteed,' states Pádraic.

'If you think about it, every baby that's ever walked or talked or learned to tie their shoe have displayed Smácht in abundance. They've paid the price. Modern marketing would prefer to have us believe however in the quick fix, the easy way out - in having desert before dinner. This applies to our health, our relationships and our businesses. Smácht as a way of working, a way of living and as a habit is just not trendy. Yet, it's the secret to all success.'

'That's why we created Smácht on Line. To provide people who have burning desires with a forum to come together; to clarify those worthy ideals; and to hold themselves accountable for achieving them. Smácht will help you achieve your goal.'

To connect with Pádraic please visit www.smacht.com or email Padraic at p@omaille.ie